easy

Microsoft® Word 2000

See it done

Do it yourself

que®

P9-EDL-412

# Copyright© 1999 by Que® Corporation

## About the Author

**Heidi Steele** is a freelance writer and software trainer. She specializes in demystifying computer concepts and making programs such as Word 2000 accessible to home users and professionals alike. Heidi Steele is the author of numerous other computer books, including *Easy Microsoft Word 97*, *How to Use the Internet*, and *How to Use Microsoft Word 97 for Windows*. She lives in Port Orchard, Washington.

**Executive Editor**
Jim Minatel

**Technical Editor**
Sherry Kinkoph

**Managing Editor**
Thomas F. Hayes

**Project Editor**
Karen S. Shields

**Copy Editor**
Victoria Elzey

**Proofreader**
John Rahm

**Indexer**
Chris Barrick

**Production Designer**
Trina Wurst

**Book Designer**
Jean Bisesi

**Cover Designer**
Anne Jones

# How to Use This Book

## It's as Easy as 1-2-3

Each part of this book is made up of a series of short, instructional lessons, designed to help you understand basic information that you need to get the most out of your computer hardware and software.

 Each step is fully illustrated to show you how it looks onscreen.

 **Click:** Click the left mouse button once.

 **Double-click:** Click the left mouse button twice in rapid succession.

 **Right-click:** Click the right mouse button once.

 **Pointer Arrow:** Highlights an item on the screen you need to point to or focus on in the step or task.

**Selection:** Highlights the area onscreen discussed in the step or task.

 **Click & Type:** Click once where indicated and begin typing to enter your text or data.

 Tips and  Warnings give you a heads-up for any extra information you may need while working through the task.

**2** Each task includes a series of quick, easy steps designed to guide you through the procedure.

**Drag**

**Drop**

**How to Drag:** Point to the starting place or object. Hold down the mouse button (right or left per instructions), move the mouse to the new location, then release the button.

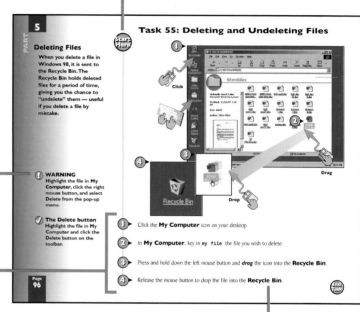

**3** Items that you select or click in menus, dialog boxes, tabs, and windows are shown in **Bold**. Information you type is in a `special font`.

 **Next Step:** If you see this symbol, it means the task you're working on continues on the next page.

 **End Task:** Task is complete.

# Easy Microsoft® Word 2000

Learning to use Word 2000 doesn't have to be an agonizing, drawn-out process. *Easy Microsoft® Word 2000* distills the key skills for you and presents them in colorful, visual steps. This book assumes that you view Word 2000 as a tool for getting your work done—no more, no less. You don't see learning a software program as an end in itself. Consequently, this book won't lead you into every nook and cranny of the program. You won't learn five ways of doing the same thing. You will, however, learn the fastest, most straightforward techniques, and you will certainly learn the shortcuts that are truly helpful.

*Easy Microsoft® Word 2000* is a book for beginners. It doesn't assume that you have ever used a word-processing program such as Word before or that you are familiar with Windows. You can use this book regardless of whether you're using Windows 95 or Windows 98.

The foundation for *Easy Microsoft® Word 2000* is many years "on the front lines" teaching Word classes to beginners. The explanations in this book have been refined in the classroom on thousands of people like you, who want to get up and running in Word without making it a lifetime project. *Easy Microsoft® Word 2000* does not merely provide stock explanations of how the program is *supposed* to work, but rather explains how it actually behaves from your viewpoint. If a particular nuance of Word behavior is confusing to most people in the classroom, it's explained here as well, on the assumption that it might be perplexing to you too.

*Easy Microsoft® Word 2000* is intended to be a both a tutorial and a reference. Feel free to flip to the exact task that you need to learn about at the moment. Of course, if you have the time, you can certainly work through the tasks sequentially, but it's not necessary to do so. You don't have to take time out from your day for "study sessions," but can instead apply the instructions in this book to your own documents, dipping into the various tasks as needed.

Word 2000 is an intuitive, powerful program, and learning to use it can (and should be) fun. Enjoy!

# Acquaint Yourself with Word 2000

Learning a new program is a bit like driving into a new town. You can guess where to find some things right away, and others you may have to putter around a while to locate. In this part, we help you with this process by taking you on a tour of the Word environment. You'll get a sense of where the various tools are and how to use them. After you know the general contours of the program, you'll be all set to delve into the specific skills required to create documents.

# Tasks

# Task 1: Starting Word 2000

## Starting Word 2000

When you want to use Word 2000 to create or revise a document, you have to ask Windows to start it for you. With Word 2000, you have several start options. You know when Word is open, even if it's hidden behind other windows, because a button bearing the Word icon appears on the **taskbar** at the bottom of your screen. An additional taskbar button appears for each Word document that you start or open.

### ✓ Why is there a paperclip in my Word window?

When you start Word, you may see a paperclip or some other animated critter sitting on one side of your Word window. This is your Office Assistant, and he's there to help you use Word and other Microsoft Office programs (see "Asking the Office Assistant for Help" later in Part 1).

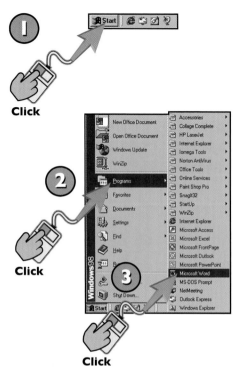

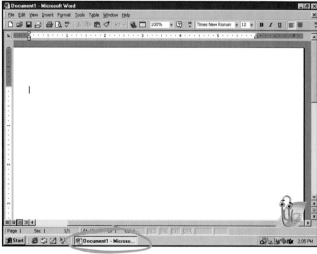

**Start Here**

① Click the **Start** button.

② Point to **Programs** in the Start menu.

③ Click **Microsoft Word**.

④ The Word window opens and a Word button appears on the taskbar.

Next Step

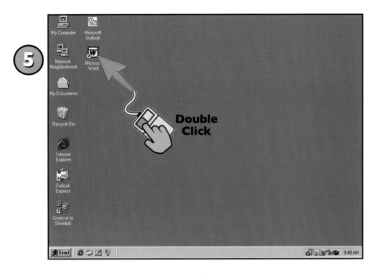

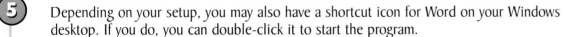

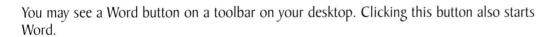

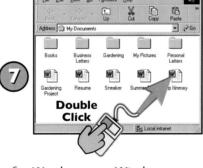

**5**    Depending on your setup, you may also have a shortcut icon for Word on your Windows desktop. If you do, you can double-click it to start the program.

**6**    You may see a Word button on a toolbar on your desktop. Clicking this button also starts Word.

**7**    You can also double-click any Word document icon, either on your Windows desktop or in a folder, to start Word and open the document.

## Resizing and Moving a Word 2000 Window

You can change the appearance of the Word window in a variety of ways. You can make it fill up the screen to give you more room to work or make it disappear temporarily so that you can see what's behind it on the Windows desktop. You can also move the Word window around on your desktop or adjust its size.

# Task 2: Working with the Word 2000 Window

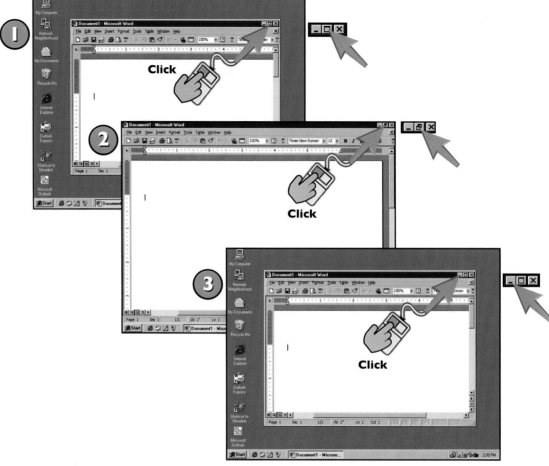

Click the **Maximize** button to make the Word window fill the screen.

The Maximize button is now a **Restore** button. Click it to return (*restore*) the window to its previous size.

Click the **Minimize** button to temporarily hide the window.

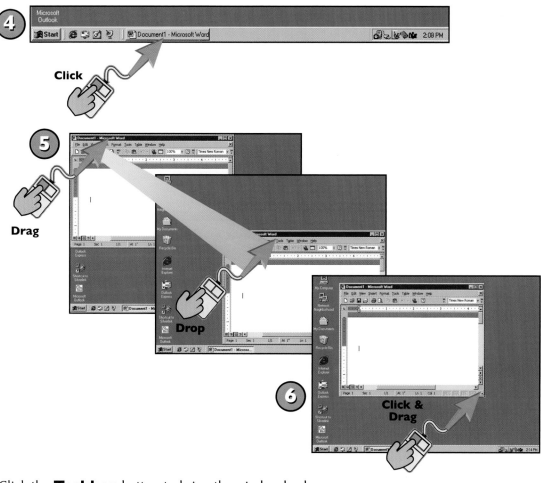

**4** Click the **Taskbar** button to bring the window back.

**5** To move the window, point to the ***title bar***, drag the window to a different location onscreen, and release the mouse button.

**6** To resize the Word window, first point to the lower-right corner of the window. The mouse pointer becomes a diagonal black arrow. Drag in the desired direction to enlarge or shrink the window.

# Task 3: Using Pull-Down Menus

## Using Pull-Down Menus

The menu bar contains nine **pull-down** menus— File, Edit, View, and so on— that contain commands for executing Word tasks. Many of these commands have equivalent buttons on the toolbars, and in most cases, it's more convenient to use the toolbar buttons than the menus. However, if you accidentally hide a toolbar or if you don't like using the mouse, you can always rely on the menus instead.

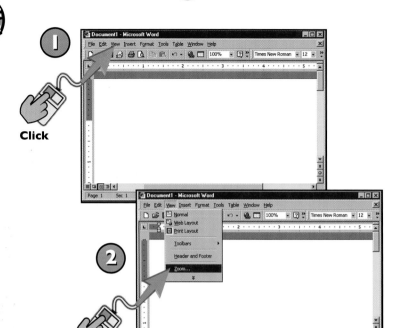

Click

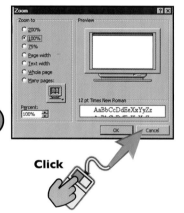

Click

### ✅ Using the keyboard instead of the mouse
If you want to use the keyboard to execute a menu command, press the **Alt** key, and then press the letter that's underlined in the menu name. For example, press **Alt+V** to pull down the View menu. Once the menu is displayed, press the underlined letter in the command you want to perform.

Click

Start Here

① Click the **View** menu to pull it down.

② Look at the **Zoom** command. It's followed by three dots (...) to show you that it leads to a dialog box. Click the command.

③ The Zoom dialog box appears. Click the **Cancel** button to close it.

Next Step

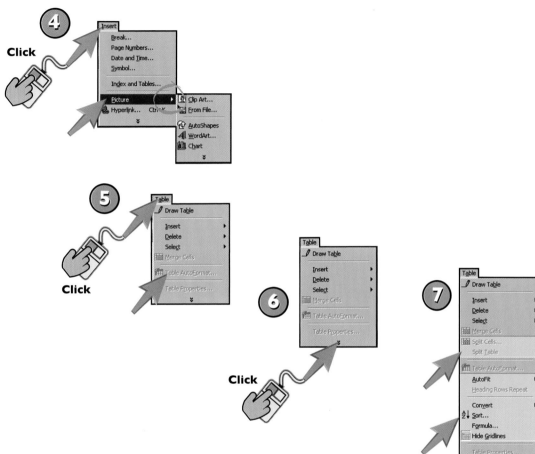

④ Click the **Insert** menu, and then point to **Picture**. The small triangle on the right of the menu command tells you that a submenu will appear. Click outside the Insert menu to close the menu.

⑤ Click the **Table** menu. The dim commands are not currently active.

⑥ Click the **Expand** arrow at the bottom of the Table menu. You can also rest your mouse pointer over the menu for a few seconds (this is called **hovering**).

⑦ The menu expands to show you all of its commands (see the next task). Click outside the menu to close it.

## Personalizing Your Menus

Word assumes that you want to use *personal menus.* When this feature is enabled, clicking a menu name displays a *short menu* that only contains the commands you use frequently. Word gives you three ways to expand the menu and display all of its commands. (You learned two ways in the previous task, and you'll learn the third here.) In this task, you practice using personal menus, and you learn how to turn off the feature if you'd rather see the full menus by default.

# Task 4: Making the Menus Your Own

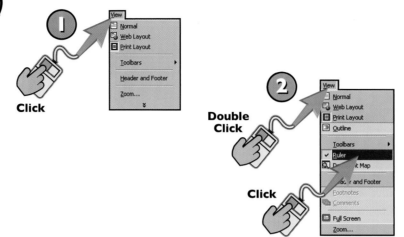

**Click**

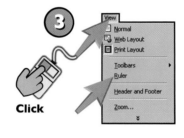

**Click**

Click the **View** menu. The short menu appears by default. Click outside of the menu to close it.

Double-click the **View** menu to quickly display the full menu. Click **Ruler**, which wasn't visible in the short menu. (See "Hiding the Ruler" later in Part I for more about the ruler.)

Click the **View** menu again. The Ruler command is now included in the short menu because you just used it. If you don't use it again for a while, it will disappear from the short menu.

To turn off personal menus, choose **Tools**, **Customize**.

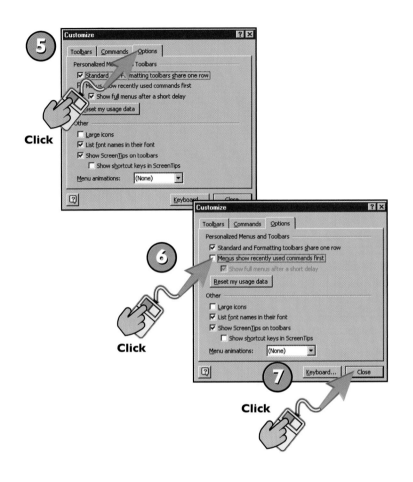

**Click**

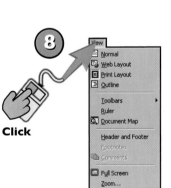

**Click**

**Click**

**Click**

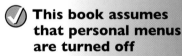

(5) Click the **Options** tab.

(6) Click the **Menus show recently used commands first** check box to clear its check mark.

(7) Click the **Close** button.

(8) Click the **View** menu a final time. Now the full menu appears by default.

✓ **This book assumes that personal menus are turned off**
The remaining tasks in this book assume that the personal menus feature is turned off. To turn it back on, repeat steps 4 through 7, but mark the **Menus show recently used commands first** check box.

End Task

# Task 5: Right-Clicking to Display Menus

## Displaying Menus On-the-Fly

In addition to using the pull-down menus at the top of the Word window, you can also use *context menus* (sometimes called *shortcut menus*). These are small menus that you display by clicking the right mouse button. The commands in a context menu vary depending on where you right-click. For example, if you right-click text, you get commands for editing and formatting text, and if you right-click a toolbar, you get a list of toolbars that you can display or hide (see "Working with Toolbars" later in Part 1 for more about toolbars). To choose a command in a context menu, use a left-click.

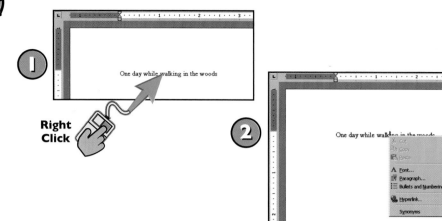

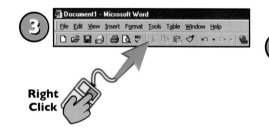

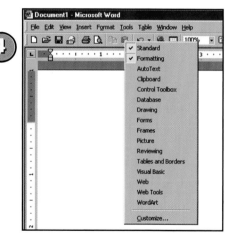

 Type a few words in your document, and then right-click anywhere on the text.

 A context menu appears with commands for working with text. Click outside the menu to close it.

 Right-click one of the toolbars.

 This time, the context menu lists your available toolbars. Click outside the menu to close it.

# Task 6: Hiding the Ruler

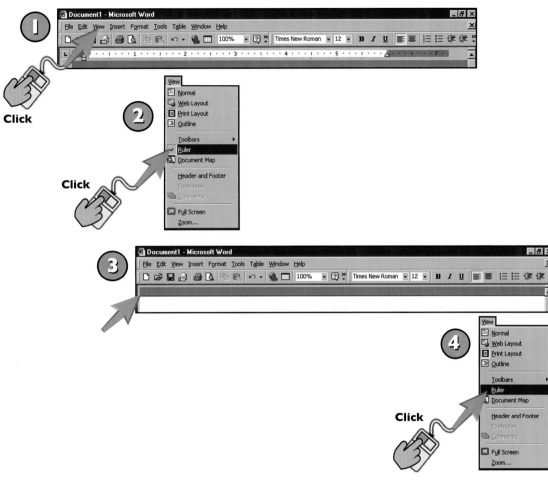

Click

Click

Click

## Hiding the Ruler

By default, a horizontal ruler appears underneath the toolbars, and a vertical ruler appears on the left edge of the document. You can use the rulers to quickly adjust tabs, indents, and margins (you'll learn about these formatting techniques in Parts 6 and 7 of this book). However, you might want to hide them so that you can see more of your document. You can easily display them again whenever you like.

1. Click **View** in the menu bar.

2. The check mark next to the Ruler command tells you that the rulers are currently displayed. Click the **Ruler** command.

3. The rulers are now hidden.

4. Choose **View**, **Ruler** again to bring the rulers back.

# Task 7: How Dialog Boxes Work

## Working with Dialog Boxes

All of Word's menu commands that are followed by ellipses (…) lead to a *dialog box*. Some dialog boxes give you options for specifying exactly what you want to do before Word actually performs the command. Once you've made your selections in a dialog box, you click the **OK** button to tell Word to carry out the command. If you decide not to go ahead with a command, you can back out of the dialog box by clicking the **Cancel** button. Here you take a quick look at the elements commonly found in dialog boxes, using the Print dialog box as an example.

Start Here

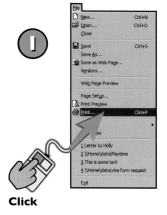
**Click**

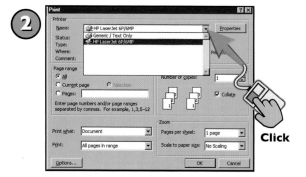
**Click**

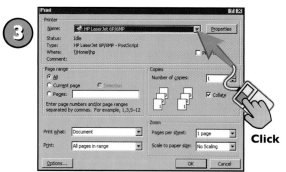
**Click**

① Choose **File**, **Print** to display the Print dialog box.

② Click the **down arrow** to the right of the Name box to display a *drop-down list*.

③ Click the **down arrow** again to hide the list without making a selection.

Next Step

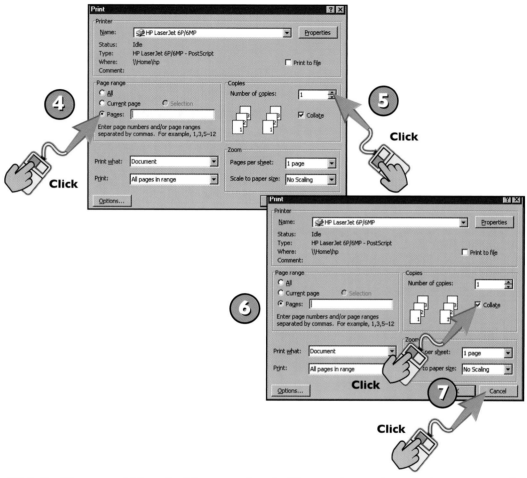

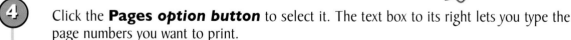

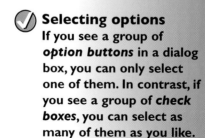

4 Click the **Pages *option button*** to select it. The text box to its right lets you type the page numbers you want to print.

5 Click the up and down ***spinner arrows*** to the right of the **Number of Copies** box to increase and decrease the number.

6 Click the **Collate *check box*** twice to clear the check box and then mark it again.

7 Click the **Cancel** button to close the Print dialog box without printing your document.

✓ **Selecting options**
If you see a group of ***option buttons*** in a dialog box, you can only select one of them. In contrast, if you see a group of ***check boxes***, you can select as many of them as you like.

End Task

# Using Word 2000 Toolbars

Word's *toolbars* contain buttons you can use to perform commonly used commands. Most people find clicking toolbar buttons more convenient than accessing commands in the pull-down menus. However, you can use any combination of toolbar buttons and menu commands you choose. Word comes with 16 toolbars. By default, it displays two of them, the Standard and Formatting toolbars. You can easily hide or display any toolbar to suit your preferences.

✓ **The Standard and Formatting toolbar buttons aren't all visible**
When the Standard and Formatting toolbars share the same row, there isn't room to display all their buttons at the same time. See the next task to learn how to bring hidden buttons into view.

# Task 8: Working with Toolbars

Start Here

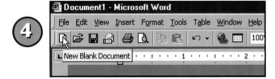

**I** By default, the Standard and Formatting toolbars share the same row. The Standard toolbar is on the left and the Formatting toolbar is on the right.

**2** The Standard toolbar contains buttons for creating, saving, and opening documents, as well as for common editing tasks.

**3** The Formatting toolbar contains buttons for formatting your text.

**4** Point to the leftmost toolbar button in the Standard toolbar. A **ScreenTip** labels the button. All the buttons have ScreenTips.

Next Step

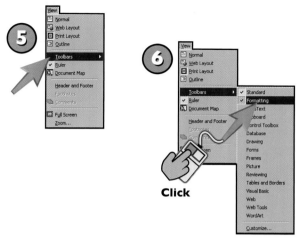

**Click**

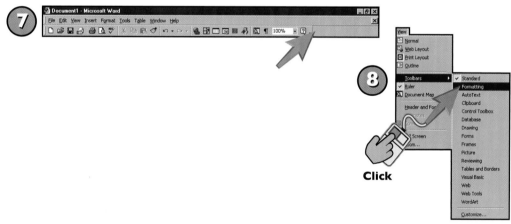

**Click**

**5** Choose **View**, **Toolbars**.

**6** Notice that the Standard and Formatting toolbars have check marks next to them. Click **Formatting**.

**7** The Formatting toolbar is now hidden.

**8** Choose **View**, **Toolbars**, and click **Formatting** again to bring the toolbar back.

End Task

## Making the Toolbars Your Own

When the Standard and Formatting toolbars are on the same row, you can't see all their toolbar buttons. Word makes it easy to access the hidden buttons, however, and as soon as you use one of them, Word moves it to a visible spot on the toolbar. In addition to displaying buttons that are included by default on a toolbar, you can also add new buttons or remove ones you never use. And, of course, you can reset a toolbar to return to the default set of buttons.

✓ **Reset your usage information**

Word tracks your usage of toolbars and personal menus and displays only the buttons and commands you use the most. To delete this record and restore the default set of visible buttons and commands, choose **Tools, Customize**, click the **Options** tab, click the **Reset Usage Data** button, click **Yes**, and click **Close**.

# Task 9: Personalizing Word 2000 Toolbars

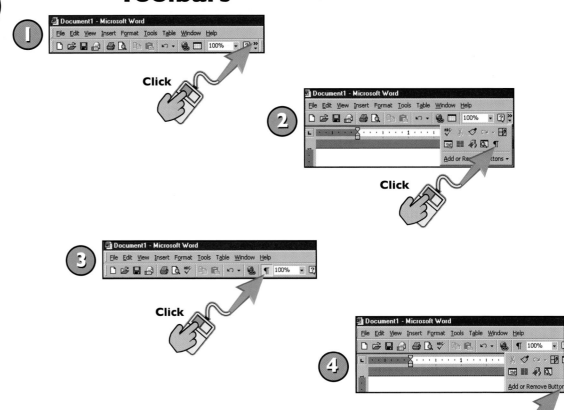

Start Here

Click

Click

Click

Click

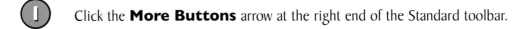

1. Click the **More Buttons** arrow at the right end of the Standard toolbar.

2. The **More Buttons** list contains the buttons that don't fit on the visible part of the toolbar. Click the **Show/Hide** button.

3. The **Show/Hide** feature is turned on and the button is now visible. Click it again to turn the **Show/Hide** feature off. (You'll learn about this button in Part 3.)

4. To add a new button to the Standard toolbar, click the **More Buttons** arrow, and then click **Add or Remove Buttons**.

Next Step

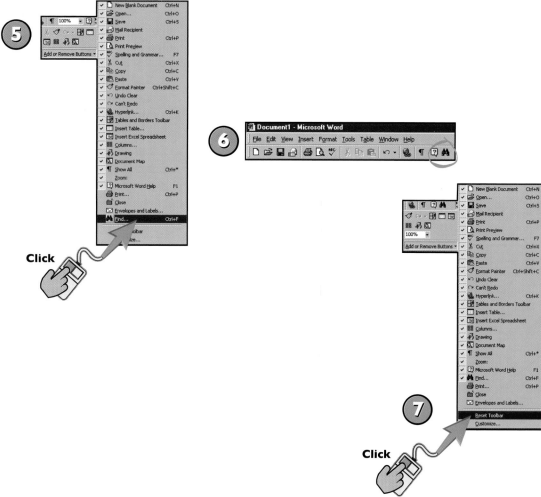

**Click**

**Click**

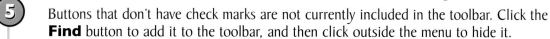

Buttons that don't have check marks are not currently included in the toolbar. Click the **Find** button to add it to the toolbar, and then click outside the menu to hide it.

The Find button is now on the Standard toolbar. (You'll learn about this feature in "Searching for Text" in Part 8.)

To reset the Standard toolbar, click the **More Buttons** arrow, click **Add or Remove Buttons**, and then click **Reset Toolbar**.

**✓ Moving buttons on a toolbar**
You can rearrange the order of the buttons on a toolbar if you like. To move a button, point to it and hold down your **Alt** key as you drag it to the desired position. Then release the **Alt** key and your mouse button at the same time.

# Task 10: Moving Your Toolbars Around

## Moving Your Toolbars Around

If you want all of the buttons in the Standard and Formatting toolbars to be visible, you can move the Formatting toolbar onto its own row. (This is the default arrangement in Word 97.) You can also drag any toolbar out on top of the Word window so that it *floats* over the window, or you can *dock* it on the left, right, or bottom edge of the window.

**Start Here**

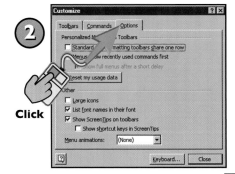

**Click**

**Click**

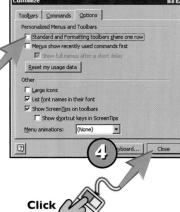

**Click**

**Click**

✓ **This book assumes that the Formatting toolbar is on its own row**
The remaining lessons in this book assume that the Formatting toolbar is positioned on its own row directly beneath the Standard toolbar.

 Choose **Tools**, **Customize**.

 In the Customize dialog box, click the **Options** tab.

 Click the **Standard and Formatting toolbars share one row** check box to clear it.

 Click the **Close** button.

Next Step

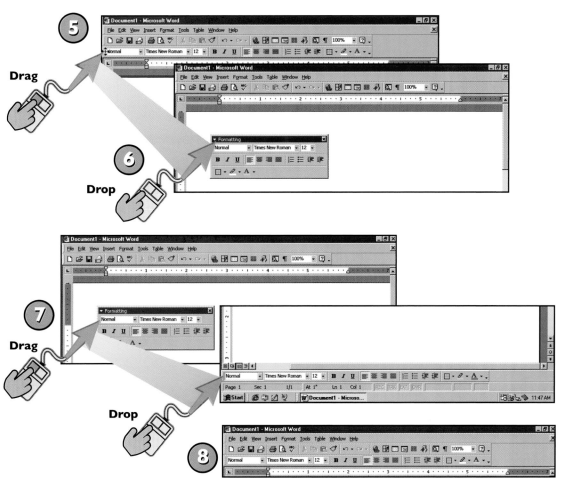

**Drag**

**Drop**

**Drag**

**Drop**

(5) The Formatting toolbar appears underneath the Standard toolbar. To move it, point to the vertical line at the left end of the toolbar.

(6) When the mouse pointer becomes a four-headed arrow, drag the toolbar into the text area of the window. If you were to release your mouse button, the toolbar would *float* over the window.

(7) Continue dragging down. When the toolbar "flattens out" along the bottom edge of the window, release the mouse button to *dock* the toolbar.

(8) Drag the Formatting toolbar back up to just beneath the Standard toolbar.

 **Docking a floating toolbar**
**If a toolbar is floating, you can quickly dock it on the edge of the window where it was most recently docked by double-clicking its title bar.**

## Using the Office Assistant

Thoughtful, friendly, and well informed, the Office Assistant helps you search Word's online help system, offers tips on how to type and format your documents more efficiently, and even provides alerts about events that require your attention, all with engaging animation and sound effects.

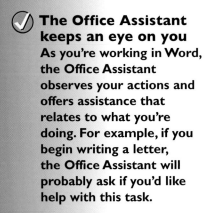

✓ **The Office Assistant keeps an eye on you**
As you're working in Word, the Office Assistant observes your actions and offers assistance that relates to what you're doing. For example, if you begin writing a letter, the Office Assistant will probably ask if you'd like help with this task.

# Task 11: Asking the Office Assistant for Help

**Click**

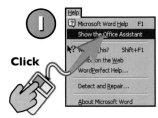

Help
② Microsoft Word Help   F1
Show the Office Assistant
⬥? W___ his?   Shift+F1
__  on the Web
WordPerfect Help...
Detect and Repair...
About Microsoft Word

②

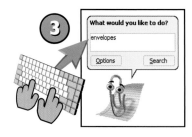

What would you like to do?

envelopes

Options     Search

③

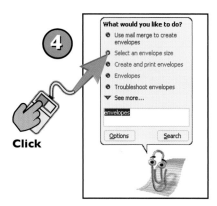

What would you like to do?
⬥ Use mail merge to create envelopes
⬥ Select an envelope size
⬥ Create and print envelopes
⬥ Envelopes
⬥ Troubleshoot envelopes
▼ See more...
envelopes
Options     Search

④

**Click**

① If you don't see the Office Assistant, choose **Help**, **Show the Office Assistant**.

② The Office Assistant, most likely a paperclip, appears onscreen. Click it to display a yellow bubble.

③ Type **envelopes** in the yellow bubble and click the **Search** button.

④ In the list of topics that appears, click **Select an envelope size**.

Next Step

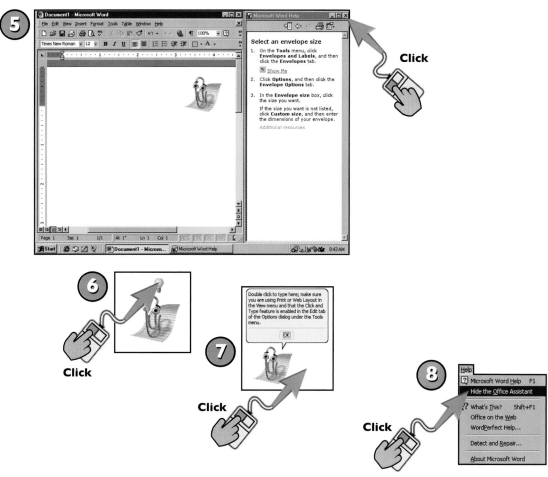

**5** The Microsoft Word Help window opens. Click its **Close** button.

**6** If you see a light bulb next to the Office Assistant, click it to display a tip.

**7** When you're finished reading the tip, click anywhere outside of the yellow bubble to close it.

**8** If you want to hide the Office Assistant, choose **Help**, **Hide the Office Assistant**.

# Task 12: Training Your Office Assistant

## Training Your Office Assistant

The Office Assistant tries its best to do your bidding, but you may want to give it a little guidance. For example, you can ask it to show you tips about keyboard shortcuts or request that it refrain from making sounds. And if you're not particularly fond of your Office Assistant's current persona, you can ask it to switch to one that better suits your personality.

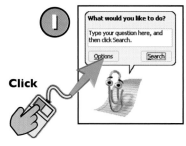

**Click**

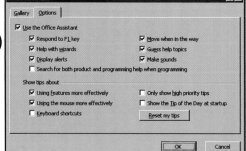

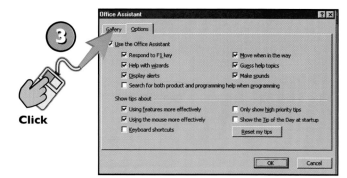

**Click**

(1) Click the Office Assistant if necessary to display the yellow bubble, and click the **Options** button.

(2) In the Options tab of the Office Assistant dialog box, mark or clear the check boxes to change your Office Assistant's behavior to better fit your needs.

(3) To switch to a different persona, click the **Gallery** tab.

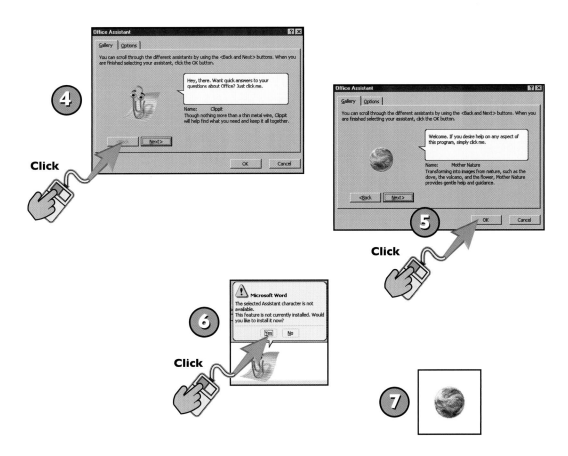

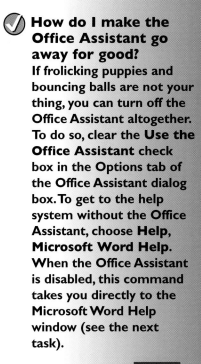

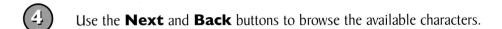

**4** Use the **Next** and **Back** buttons to browse the available characters.

**5** When you find one that you like, click **OK**.

**6** If you see a message stating that this feature is not currently installed, insert your Office 2000 CD-ROM, and click **Yes**.

**7** The new assistant now appears in your Word window.

**How do I make the Office Assistant go away for good?**
If frolicking puppies and bouncing balls are not your thing, you can turn off the Office Assistant altogether. To do so, clear the **Use the Office Assistant** check box in the **Options** tab of the Office Assistant dialog box. To get to the help system without the Office Assistant, choose **Help, Microsoft Word Help**. When the Office Assistant is disabled, this command takes you directly to the Microsoft Word Help window (see the next task).

# Task 13: Getting Help from the Help Menu

## Working with the Help Window

Whether the Office Assistant leads you to the Microsoft Word Help window or you get there on your own, becoming familiar with this window will help you get the answers you need without pestering your coworkers or family members. The Microsoft Word Help window is divided into two panes. When you access it through the Office Assistant, the window is "collapsed" to only show the right pane. In this task, you temporarily disable the Office Assistant so that you can get to the help window directly, and then you learn how to use the left pane to search for information.

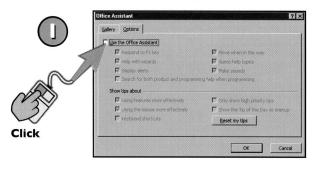

Click

Click

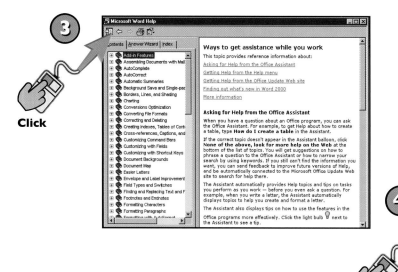

Click

Click

1. Turn off the Office Assistant by clearing the **Use the Office Assistant** check box in the Office Assistant dialog box and clicking **OK** (see the previous task).

2. Choose **Help, Microsoft Word Help** to display the Microsoft Word Help window.

3. Click the **Hide** button to hide the left pane, and then click the **Show** button (which replaces the Hide button) to display it again.

4. Click the **Contents** tab in the left pane, and then click the plus sign next to any of the topics.

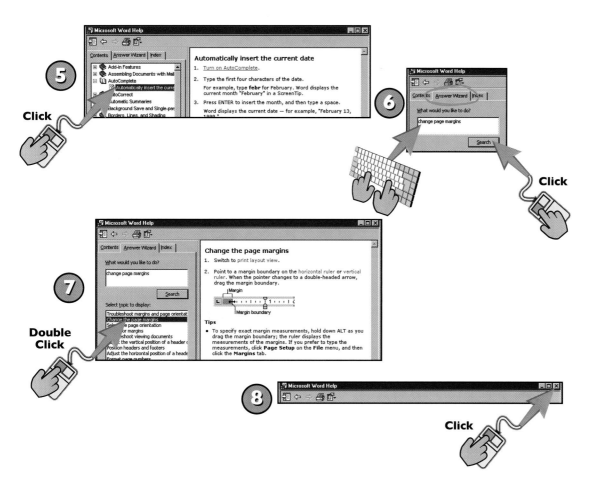

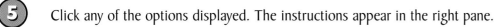

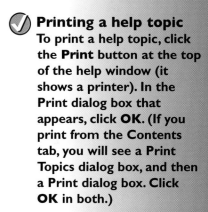

**Printing a help topic**
To print a help topic, click the **Print** button at the top of the help window (it shows a printer). In the Print dialog box that appears, click **OK**. (If you print from the Contents tab, you will see a Print Topics dialog box, and then a Print dialog box. Click **OK** in both.)

**Navigating around the Help topics**
To move back and forth among the help topics you've displayed since opening the help window this time, click the **Back** and **Forward** buttons (the left and right arrows) at the top of the window.

(5) Click any of the options displayed. The instructions appear in the right pane.

(6) Click the **Answer Wizard** tab in the left pane. Type **change page margins**, and click the **Search** button.

(7) In the topics that appear, double-click **Change the page margins**. The instructions appear in the right pane.

(8) Click the **Close** button to exit the help window. (To turn on the Office Assistant again, choose **Help**, **Show the Office Assistant**.)

End Task

# Task 14: Exiting Word 2000

## Exiting Word 2000

**When you are finished working with Word, you need to exit the program. When you issue the command to exit, Word checks to see if you are working on a document that has unsaved changes. If you are, it gives you a chance to save the document before closing it. As soon as you exit Word, the buttons for the Word documents that you had open disappear from the taskbar to let you know that the program is no longer running. In this task, you learn to close Word with the File, Exit command and with the Close button.**

Start Here

Click

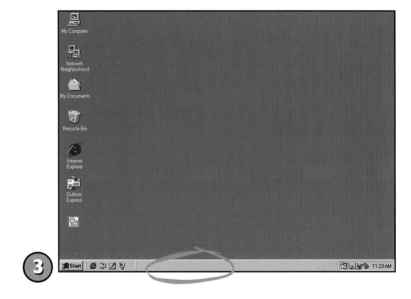

**1**   Choose **File**, **Exit**.

**2**   If Word asks whether to save changes to a document, click **Yes** or **No** (see "Saving a Document" in Part 4). (If the Office Assistant is hidden, you'll see a message box asking this same question.)

**3**   All open Word windows close, and no Word buttons remain on the taskbar.

Next Step

**4**

**5**

**6**

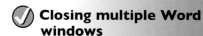

**4** If you have only one Word document open, you will have two Close buttons. Click the top **Close** button as a shortcut for choosing File, Exit.

**5** Click the lower **Close** button if you only want to close the document, but leave the Word window open.

**6** If you have more than one Word document open, you will only have one **Close** button in each window. Clicking this button closes the active Word window, but leaves the others open.

✓ **Closing multiple Word windows**
With Word 2000, if you open more than one document at a time, it displays each one in a separate Word window. Choosing File, Exit in any Word window closes them all.

End Task

# Entering Text

Even if you have never used a word-processing program before, you'll feel comfortable typing text in Word in no time. In this part, you learn typing basics, such basics as when to press Enter and how to move around the document. You also find out how to insert new text into text you have already typed, and how to track down a document that you may have misplaced.

# Tasks

# Task 1: Entering Text

## Typing Text

Typing text in a Word document is simple. As soon as you start Word, you can begin typing in the blank document that appears. You don't have to worry about leaving room for margins. Word assumes that you're typing on 8 1/2-by 11-inch paper, with 1-inch margins on the top and bottom and 1 1/4-inch margins on the left and right. If you're typing a paragraph more than one line long, do not press Enter at the end of the lines. Word wraps the text from line to line for you.

✓ **The mouse pointer and the insertion point**
The mouse pointer, called the *I-beam*, is often confused with the insertion point. The insertion point (sometimes called the *cursor*) shows you where your text will appear when you type. The I-beam just lets you move the insertion point around the document (see the next two tasks).

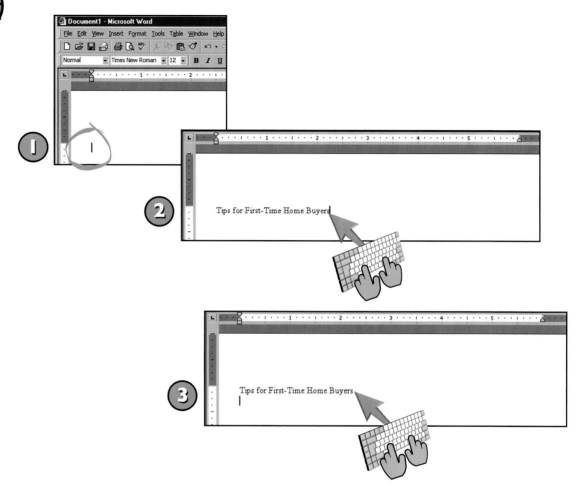

**Start Here**

1. Start Word. The flashing vertical bar you see in the blank document is called the *insertion point*.

2. As you type, the insertion point shows you where the next character will be inserted.

3. When you want to end a short line of text (a short paragraph), press **Enter**. The insertion point moves to the next line.

Next Step

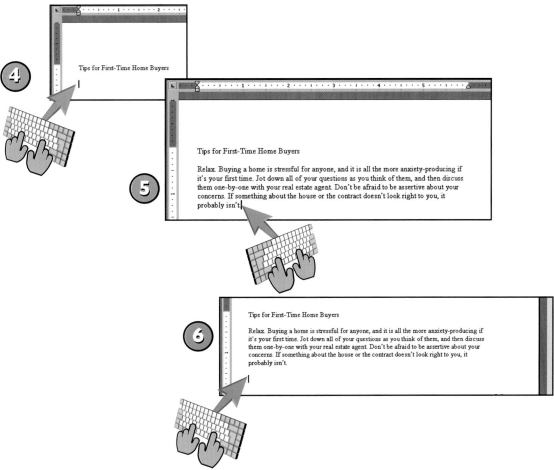

(4) When the insertion point is on a new line, pressing **Enter** creates a blank line.

(5) When you type a paragraph that is more than one line long, you should not press **Enter** at the end of the lines within the paragraph.

(6) You should press **Enter** when you're at the end of the paragraph, or press **Enter** twice if you want to add a blank line.

 **Correcting mistakes as you're typing**
If you type the wrong character accidentally, you can press the **Backspace** key to delete it. You'll learn more about how to delete text in "Deleting Text" in Part 3.

## Using the Mouse to Move Around

**As soon as you've typed some text in a blank document, you need to know how to move the insertion point around within the text to make editing changes. You can move the insertion point by clicking the mouse or by pressing navigation keys on the keyboard. In this task and the next, you learn how to navigate with the mouse. Experiment a little to see which methods you like the best.**

# Task 2: Moving Around the Document with the Mouse

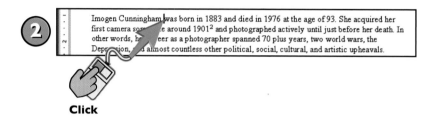

Imogen Cunningham was born in 1883 and died in 1976 at the age of 93. She acquired her first camera sometime around 1901[2] and photographed actively until just before her death. In other words, her career as a photographer spanned 70 plus years, two world wars, the Depression, and almost countless other political, social, cultural, and artistic upheavals.

Imogen Cunningham was born in 1883 and died in 1976 at the age of 93. She acquired her first camera sometime around 1901[2] and photographed actively until just before her death. In other words, her career as a photographer spanned 70 plus years, two world wars, the Depression, and almost countless other political, social, cultural, and artistic upheavals.

**Click**

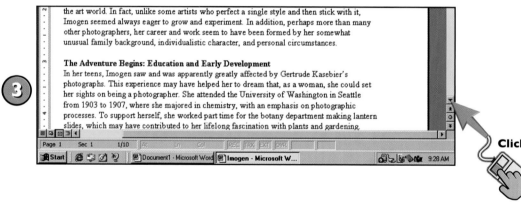

the art world. In fact, unlike some artists who perfect a single style and then stick with it, Imogen seemed always eager to grow and experiment. In addition, perhaps more than many other photographers, her career and work seem to have been formed by her somewhat unusual family background, individualistic character, and personal circumstances.

**The Adventure Begins: Education and Early Development**
In her teens, Imogen saw and was apparently greatly affected by Gertrude Kasebier's photographs. This experience may have helped her to dream that, as a woman, she could set her sights on being a photographer. She attended the University of Washington in Seattle from 1903 to 1907, where she majored in chemistry, with an emphasis on photographic processes. To support herself, she worked part time for the botany department making lantern slides, which may have contributed to her lifelong fascination with plants and gardening.

Page 1    Sec 1    1/10    At    Ln    Col    REC TRK EXT OVR

Start    Document1 - Microsoft Word    Imogen - Microsoft W...    9:28 AM

**Click**

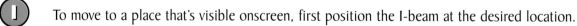

To move to a place that's visible onscreen, first position the I-beam at the desired location.

Then click. The insertion point moves to the new location.

Click the down scroll arrow on the **scrollbar** to bring the lower part of a long document into view.

Next Step

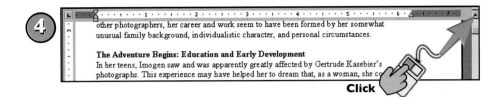

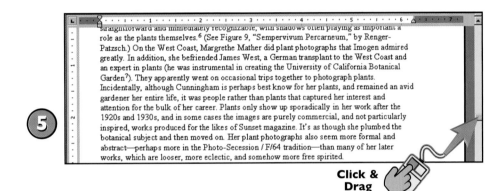

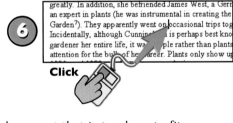

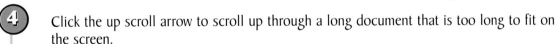

(4) Click the up scroll arrow to scroll up through a long document that is too long to fit on the screen.

(5) Point to the **scroll box** and drag it up or down the scrollbar to move quickly through a long document.

(6) After you've scrolled through the document, remember to click to move the insertion point before you start typing.

# Task 3: Typing Anywhere on the Page

## Using Click and Type

Word 2000 introduced *click and type.* This feature lets you start typing in the middle of the page or on the right margin by simply double-clicking at the desired location. You don't have to insert tabs first or change your alignment; Word handles this for you (see Part 6 for more about these formatting options). The examples in this task show how you could use click and type to quickly type a phone list.

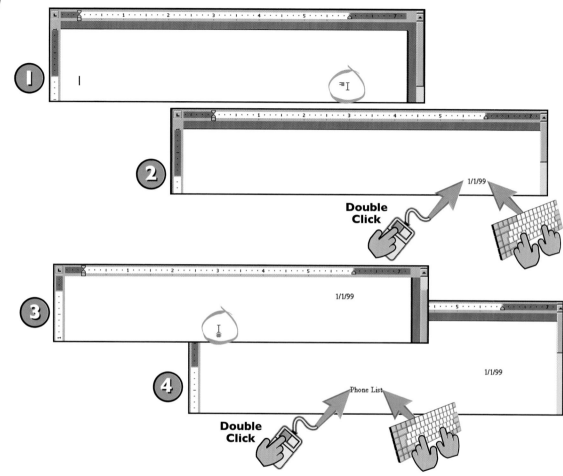

Start Here

Double Click

Double Click

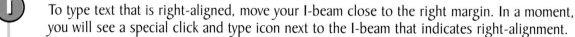

✅ **Click and type isn't working**

Click and type only works in Print Layout view. If double-clicking doesn't move the insertion point, first choose **View, Print Layout.** Then choose **Tools, Options.** Click the **Edit** tab, make sure the **Enable click and type** check box is marked, and click **OK.**

① To type text that is right-aligned, move your I-beam close to the right margin. In a moment, you will see a special click and type icon next to the I-beam that indicates right-alignment.

② Double-click to move the insertion point and type your text.

③ To type text that is centered, move your I-beam to the center of the page. The I-beam icon changes to indicate center alignment.

④ Double-click to move the insertion point and type your text.

Next Step

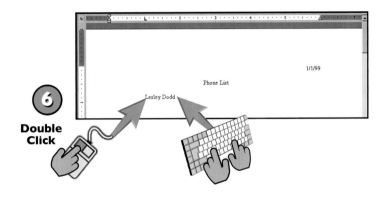

**Double
Click**

(5) To type text that is left-aligned, move your I-beam to the spot where you want to begin typing (not at the center or at the right margin). The I-beam icon changes to show left-alignment.

(6) Double-click to move the insertion point and type your text.

End
Task

## Using the Keyboard to Move Around

You might find it faster to navigate with the keyboard because then you don't have to take your hands away from the keys. When navigating with the mouse, you must constantly move your hands away from the keyboard to the mouse and back. When you navigate with the keyboard, the insertion point moves as you press the keys. You don't have to click once before you start typing to move the insertion point, as you do when you navigate with the mouse.

 **Pressing key combinations**
When you press a key combination such as Ctrl+Home, make sure to hold down the first key as you press the second key, and then release both keys.

# Task 4: Moving Around the Document with the Keyboard

 ← or →

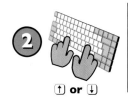

↑ or ↓

Ctrl+← or Ctrl+→

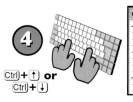

Ctrl+↑ or Ctrl+↓

 Press the **left-** and **right-arrow** keys to move one character to the left or to the right.

 Press the **up-** and **down-arrow** keys to move one line up or down.

 Press **Ctrl+left arrow** and **Ctrl+right arrow** to move one word to the left or to the right.

 Press **Ctrl+up arrow** and **Ctrl+down arrow** to move one paragraph up or down.

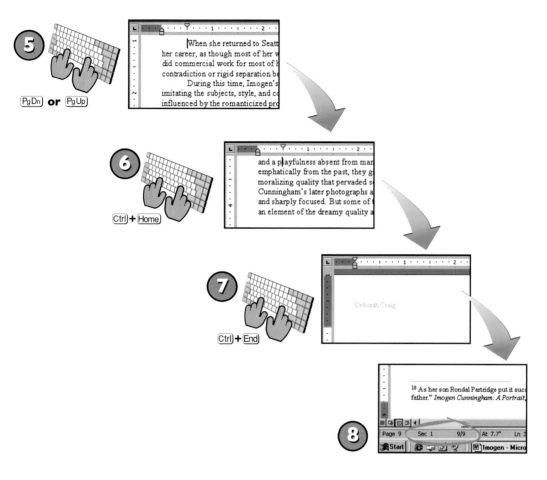

**5** Press **Page Down** and **Page Up** to move one screenful of text down or up.

**6** Press **Ctrl+Home** to move to the very beginning of the document.

**7** Press **Ctrl+End** to move to the very end of the document.

**8** You can always tell what page you're on by looking at the *status bar*. Here, the insertion point is on page 9 of a 9-page document.

# Task 5: Going to a Specific Page

## Finding a Specific Page

When you're editing a long document, you often need to go to a particular page to make a change. You can, of course, navigate to that page using the standard mouse and keyboard techniques described in the previous two tasks. However, it's often faster to use Word's *Go To* feature, which allows you to jump directly to any page in your document.

Start Here

**Click**

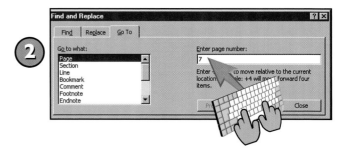

**②**

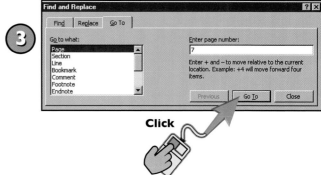

**③**

**Click**

### ✓ Using Go To to make changes

You can use the Go To feature to make editing changes on several pages. Jump to the first page, click outside of the dialog box to deactivate it, and make the change in the text. Then click the title bar of the dialog box to reactivate it and jump to the next page, and so on.

**①** Choose **Edit, Go To** to display the **Go To** tab of the Find and Replace dialog box.

**②** Type the number of the page in the **Enter page number** text box.

**③** Click the **Go To** button.

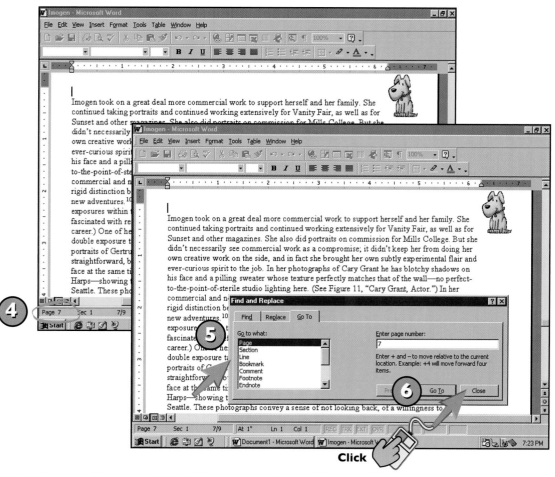

**Click**

**4** Word jumps to that page. (Check the page number in the status bar.)

**5** The dialog box remains onscreen so that you can go to another page.

**6** When you're finished using Go To, click the **Close** button.

End Task

# Task 6: Inserting Text

## Inserting Text

As you're typing a document, you'll no doubt need to go back and add some text here and there. Inserting text is an extremely straightforward task. When you type new text, Word pushes the existing text out of the way to make room for it. Depending on the exact location of the insertion point when you start typing, you will either need to add a space at the beginning of the insertion or at the end.

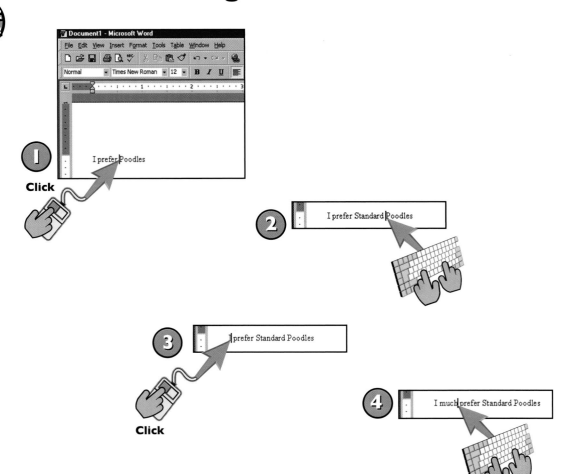

**Start Here**

**Click**

**Click**

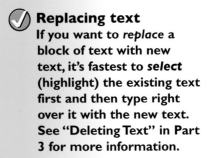

### ✓ Replacing text

If you want to *replace* a block of text with new text, it's fastest to *select* (highlight) the existing text first and then type right over it with the new text. See "Deleting Text" in Part 3 for more information.

**1** To insert text between two words that you have already typed, move the insertion point to just before the first letter of the second word.

**2** Type your text, and press the **Spacebar**.

**3** You can also move the insertion point to just after the first word.

**4** If you do this, you will need to press the **Spacebar** first, and then type your text.

**End Task**

# Task 7: Combining and Splitting Paragraphs

**1** We are looking for a home for a stray puppy we took in last week. We're guessing that she is about six months old. Jessie (her temporary name) looks like an Australian Shepherd mix. She has a thick gray, brown, and white coat and soft, floppy ears. Yesterday, we took her to the vet for a check-up and her first series of shots.

The vet said she is in great shape, but is a little underweight and has a mild ear infection. Not too bad for a puppy who was wandering around the streets of Seattle by herself! If you are interested in adopting her, please give us a call at 555-4345.

**Click**

**2** We are looking for a home for a stray puppy we took in last week. We're guessing that she is about six months old. Jessie (her temporary name) looks like an Australian Shepherd mix. She has a thick gray, brown, and white coat and soft, floppy ears. Yesterday, we took her to the vet for a check-up and her first series of shots. The vet said she is in great shape, but is a little underweight and has a mild ear infection. Not too bad for a puppy who was wandering around the streets of Seattle by herself! If you interested in adopting her, please give us a call at 555-4345.

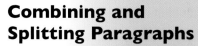

**3** We are looking for a home for a stray puppy we took in last week. We're guessing that she is about six months old. Jessie (her temporary name) looks like an Australian Shepherd mix. She has a thick gray, brown, and white coat and soft, floppy ears. Yesterday, we took her to the vet for a check-up and her first series of shots. The vet said she is in great shape, but is a little underweight and has a mild ear infection. Not too bad for a puppy who was wandering around the streets of Seattle by herself! If you are interested in adopting her, please give us a call at 555-4345.

**Click**

**4** We are looking for a home for a stray puppy we took in last week. We're guessing that she is about six months old. Jessie (her temporary name) looks like an Australian Shepherd mix. She has a thick gray, brown, and white coat and soft, floppy ears.

Yesterday, we took her to the vet for a check-up and her first series of shots. The vet said she is in great shape, but is a little underweight and has a mild ear infection. Not too bad for a puppy who was wandering around the streets of Seattle by herself! If you are interested in adopting her, please give us a call at 555-4345.

## Combining and Splitting Paragraphs

**When you're composing a new document, you'll most often revise the paragraph structure as you go. You may need to combine shorter paragraphs into one longer one or break up a long paragraph into two or more shorter ones. You can adjust the breaks between paragraphs by using only the Enter and the Backspace keys.**

**1** To join two paragraphs, move the insertion point to the beginning of the second paragraph.

**2** Press the **Backspace** key once to join the paragraphs (or twice if there is a blank line between the paragraphs). You may then need to press the **Spacebar** to add a space at the insertion point.

**3** To split one paragraph into two, move the insertion point to just before the first letter of what will become the new paragraph.

**4** Press **Enter** once, or twice if you want a blank line between the paragraphs.

# Editing Text

Word processing programs would be worthless if we couldn't use them to revise text. Indeed, the most valuable aspect of using Word is that you can quickly and painlessly edit text that you've already typed. The skills you learn here—selecting (highlighting) text, deleting text, cutting and pasting text, undoing actions, and so on—form the foundation for everything else you'll do in Word.

# Tasks

# Task 1: Selecting Text with the Mouse

## Use the Mouse to Select Text

*Selecting* (or highlighting) text is an essential word-processing skill. In many cases, you have to select text before performing a command so Word knows what text you want to affect. For example, you have to select text before cutting and pasting or applying many kinds of formatting. In this task, you learn how to select text using the mouse (the next task teaches you how to select with the keyboard). Steps 1 and 2 show you the most basic way of selecting text. Steps 3 through 6 illustrate some shortcuts for selecting specific amounts of text.

Start Here!

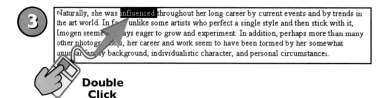

**①** Naturally, she was influenced throughout her long career by current events and by trends in the art world. In fact, unlike some artists who perfect a single style and then stick with it, Imogen seemed always eager to grow and experiment. In addition, perhaps more than many other photographers, her career and work seem to have been formed by her somewhat unusual family background, individualistic character, and personal circumstance.

**Click & Drag**

**②** Naturally, she was influenced throughout her long career by current events and by trends in the art world. In fact, unlike some artists who perfect a single style and then stick with it, Imogen seemed always eager to grow and experiment. In addition, perhaps more than many other photographers, her career and work seem to have been formed by her somewhat unusual family background, individualistic character, and personal circumstance.

**Click**

**③** Naturally, she was influenced throughout her long career by current events and by trends in the art world. In fact, unlike some artists who perfect a single style and then stick with it, Imogen seemed always eager to grow and experiment. In addition, perhaps more than many other photographers, her career and work seem to have been formed by her somewhat unusual family background, individualistic character, and personal circumstance.

**Double Click**

**①** Position the I-beam at one end of the text you want to select. Drag to the other end of the text, and then release the mouse button.

**②** If you selected the wrong amount of text, deselect it by clicking anywhere in the document.

**③** To select an individual word, double-click it.

Next Step

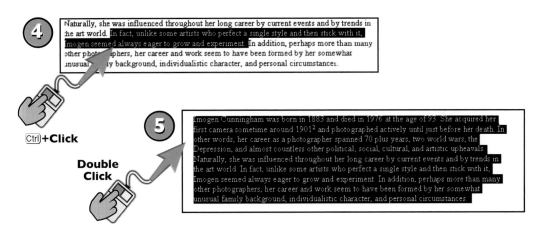

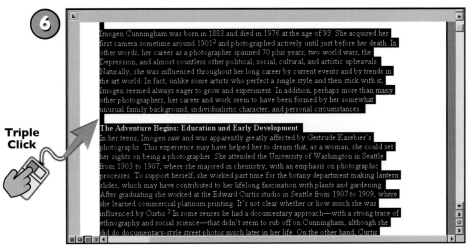

To select a single sentence, hold down the **Ctrl** key as you click anywhere on the sentence.

To select a paragraph, move the mouse pointer to the left of the paragraph and double-click.

To select the entire document, move the mouse pointer to the left of the text and triple-click.

**Ctrl**+Click

**Double Click**

**Triple Click**

! **Warning**
If you have released the mouse button after selecting a block of text, you can't adjust the amount of text that's selected by pointing to it and dragging. If you try to do this, you'll end up *moving* the text instead. You can, however, adjust the selection by using the keyboard (see the next task). If you want to use the mouse to adjust the selection, click once to deselect the text, and then select it again.

! **Warning**
As you'll see in "Deleting Text" later in Part 3, when text is selected, any text you type *replaces* the selected text. If you don't want this to happen, deselect the text before typing.

# Task 2: Selecting Text with the Keyboard

## Use the Keyboard to Select Text

Although you'll probably use the mouse to select text most of the time, you may occasionally want to use the keyboard. If you only want to select a few characters, it's usually easiest to use the keyboard. You can also use the keyboard to adjust the size of a selection you initially made with the mouse. (As mentioned in the preceding task, you can't adjust a selection with the mouse after you've released the mouse button.) The first five steps describe keyboard-only techniques. The last step shows you a method using the keyboard and the mouse together.

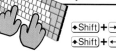

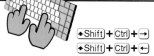

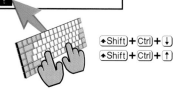

Relax. Buying a home is stressful for anyone, and it is all the more anxiety producing if it's your first time. Jot down all of your questions as you think of them, and then discuss them one-by-one with your real estate agent.
Don't be afraid to be assertive about your concerns. If something about the house or the contract doesn't look right to you, it probably isn't.

➀ **Shift** + **→**
  **Shift** + **←**

➁ **Shift** + **Ctrl** + **→**
  **Shift** + **Ctrl** + **←**

➂ **Shift** + **Ctrl** + **↓**
  **Shift** + **Ctrl** + **↑**

➀ Press **Shift+Right arrow** to select character by character to the right, or **Shift+Left arrow** to select to the left.

➁ Press **Shift+Ctrl+Right arrow** to select word by word to the right, or **Shift+Ctrl+Left arrow** to select to the left.

➂ Press **Shift+Ctrl+Down arrow** to select down paragraph by paragraph, or **Shift+Ctrl+Up arrow** to select up.

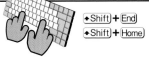

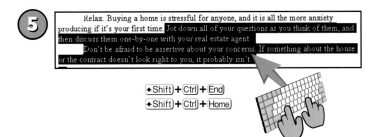

+Shift + End
+Shift + Home

+Shift + Ctrl + End
+Shift + Ctrl + Home

+Shift + **Click**

**Click**

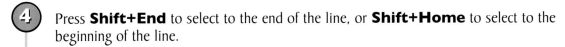

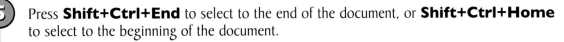

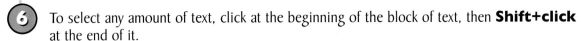

④ Press **Shift+End** to select to the end of the line, or **Shift+Home** to select to the beginning of the line.

⑤ Press **Shift+Ctrl+End** to select to the end of the document, or **Shift+Ctrl+Home** to select to the beginning of the document.

⑥ To select any amount of text, click at the beginning of the block of text, then **Shift+click** at the end of it.

✅ **Multiple key combinations**
With the keyboard methods that involve pressing the Shift and/or Ctrl key with one of the arrow keys, just keep the Shift and/or Ctrl key held down as you press the arrow keys repeatedly to continue selecting character by character, word by word, and so on.

End
Task

# Task 3: Deleting Text

## Deleting Text

It's as important to know how to delete text as to insert it. In this task, you learn techniques for deleting that you'll use every time you edit a document.

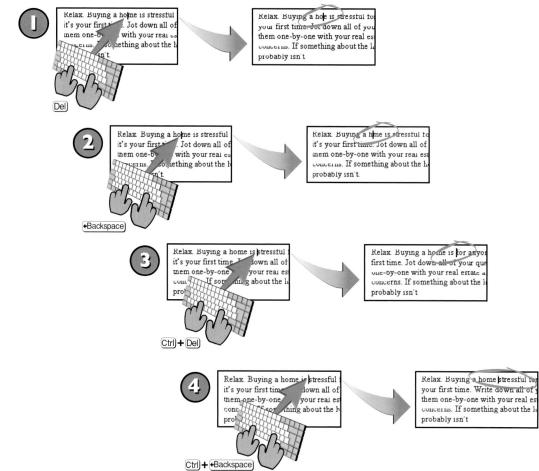

✓ **Deleting several words simultaneously**
To delete several words at once, just hold down the Ctrl key as you press the Delete or Backspace key repeatedly.

✓ **Restoring deleted text**
If you delete text accidentally, you can use the Undo feature to get it back. See the next task to learn how.

① Press the **Delete** key to delete the character to the right of the insertion point.

② Press the **Backspace key** to delete the character to the left.

③ Press **Ctrl+Delete** to delete the word to the right of the insertion point.

④ Press **Ctrl+Backspace** to delete the word to the left.

Relax. Buying a home is stressful for anyone, and it is all the more anxiety-producing if it's your first time. Jot down all of your questions as you think of them, and then discuss them one-by-one with your real estate agent. Don't be afraid to be assertive about your concerns. If something about the house or the contract doesn't look right to you, it probably isn't

Relax. Buying a home is stressful for anyone, and it is all the more anxiety-producing if it's your first time. Don't be afraid to be assertive about your concerns. If something about the house or the contract doesn't look right to you, it probably isn't.

[Del]

Relax. Buying a home is stressful for anyone, and it is all the more anxiety-producing if it's your first time. Jot down all of your questions as you think of them, and then discuss them one-by-one with your real estate agent. Don't be afraid to be assertive about your concerns. If something about the house or the contract doesn't look right to you, it probably isn't

Relax. Buying a home is stressful for anyone, and it is all the more anxiety-producing if it's your first time. Write down all of your questions as you think of them, and then discuss them one-by-one with your real estate agent. Don't be afraid to be assertive about your concerns. If something about the house or the contract doesn't look right to you, it probably isn't

(5) To delete a block of text, first select the text.

(6) Then press the **Delete** key.

(7) To replace existing text with text you type, first select the existing text.

(8) Then type the new text.

# Task 4: Undoing Mistakes

## Using Undo

Word lets you undo most actions, including typing, deleting, moving, copying, and formatting text. One of the best aspects of Word's Undo feature is that it allows you to undo multiple actions, not just your most recent one. As you experiment with Undo, keep in mind that there are some actions Word cannot undo, such as opening, saving, or printing a document.

Start Here

**①** Buying a home is stressful for anyone, and it is all the more anxiety-producing if it's your first time. Jot down all of your questions as you think of them, and then discuss them one-by-one with your real estate agent. Don't be afraid to be assertive about your concerns. If something doesn't look right to you, it probably isn't

**②** Buying a home is stressful for anyone, and it is all the more anxiety-producing if it's your first time. Jot down all of your questions as you think of them, and then discuss them one-by-one with your real estate agent. Don't be afraid to be assertive about your concerns. If something doesn't look right to you, it probably isn't

**③** Buying a home is stressful for anyone, and it is all the more anxiety-producing if it's your first time. Don't be afraid to be assertive about your concerns. If something doesn't look right to you, it probably isn't.

Del

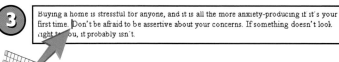
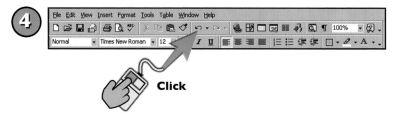

**④**

Click

**①** To practice using Undo, start Word and type a little text.

**②** Select some of the text that you typed.

**③** Press **Delete** to remove it.

**④** Click the **Undo** button on the Standard toolbar. (Click the button itself, not the down arrow to its right.)

Next Step

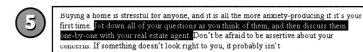

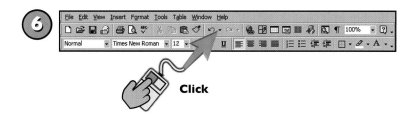

**Click**

**Click**

✅ **Using the Redo button**
To the right of the Undo
button on the Standard
toolbar is the Redo button.
Click this button if you
have used Undo to reverse
an action and then decide
that you want to perform
the action after all.

5️⃣ Word restores the deleted text. If you keep clicking the **Undo** button, Word reverses
previous actions one by one.

6️⃣ To undo several actions at once, first click the **down arrow** to the right of the Undo
button.

7️⃣ Then click any action in the list that appears to undo everything back to, and including, that
action.

✅ **Undoing actions with
a keyboard shortcut**
The keyboard shortcut for
clicking the Undo button is
Ctrl+Z. If you keep
pressing Ctrl+Z, Word
undoes actions one by one.

**PART 3**

# Task 5: Moving Text

Start Here

## Moving Text

What most people especially appreciate about writing with a word-processing program is the ability to *cut and paste* text from one place in your document to another. In this task, you learn how to *cut* (move) text. When you perform a cut, you remove the text from one location and paste it into another. In the next task, you learn how to *copy* text. Copying leaves the text in its current location and places a duplicate of that text somewhere else.

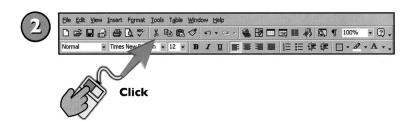

Click

1. Select the text that you want to cut.

2. Click the **Cut** button on the Standard toolbar.

3. The text disappears from the document.

Next Step

We are looking for a home for a stray puppy we took in last week. We're guessing that she is about six months old. Jessie (her temporary name) looks like an Australian Shepherd mix. She has a thick brown, and white coat and soft, floppy ear.

**Click**

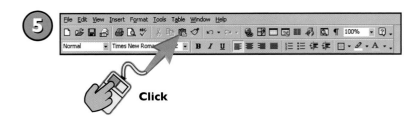

File Edit View Insert Format Tools Table Window Help

Normal | Times New Roma

**Click**

We are looking for a home for a stray puppy we took in last week. We're guessing that she is about six months old. Jessie (her temporary name) looks like an Australian Shepherd mix. She has a thick brown, gray, and white coat and soft, floppy ear.

④ Move the insertion point to the place where you want to move the text.

⑤ Click the **Paste** button on the Standard toolbar.

⑥ The text is moved to the new location.

 **Cutting and pasting with keyboard shortcuts**
If you'd rather use the keyboard to cut and paste text, click **Ctrl+X** in step 2 to execute the Cut command, and **Ctrl+V** in step 5 to execute the Paste command.

# Task 6: Copying Text

## Copying Text

**Copying text can save you a lot of typing time. If you have a block of text in one place in your document that you want to use somewhere else, it's much faster to copy it than to type it again. The steps here show you how to copy text from one location to another within the same document.**

✓ **Copying text from one document to another**
If you want to copy text into another document, open the document containing the text (the source) and the one to which you want to copy the text (the target). (See "Opening a Document" in Part 4.) Follow the steps shown here, with one variation: In step 4, click the taskbar button for the target document, and move the insertion point to the desired location in that document. Then continue with the remaining steps.

**1** Last week, we noticed our ten-month old puppy Max was limping, so we took him to the vet. It turns out that he has Eosinophilic Panosteitis ("growing pains"). is a disease of puppies between five and twelve months of age.

**2**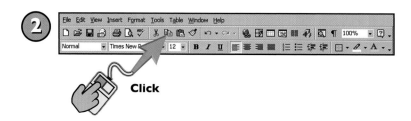

**Click**

**3** Last week, we noticed our ten-month old puppy Max was limping, so we took him to the vet. It turns out that he has Eosinophilic Panosteitis ("growing pains"). is a disease of puppies between five and twelve months of age.

**1** Select the text that you want to copy.

**2** Click the **Copy** button on the Standard toolbar.

**3** The selected text remains in its current location because you're copying it, not moving it.

Last week, we noticed our ten-month old puppy Max was limping, so we took him to the vet. It turns out that he has Eosinophilic Panosteitis ("growing pains"). Is a disease of puppies between five and twelve months of age.

**Click**

File Edit View Insert Format Tools Table Window Help

Normal     Times New Rom... 2     B I U

**Click**

Last week, we noticed our ten-month old puppy Max was limping, so we took him to the vet. It turns out that he has Eosinophilic Panosteitis ("growing pains"). Eosinophilic Panosteitis is a disease of puppies between five and twelve months of age.

✔ **Copying and pasting with keyboard shortcuts**
To copy and paste with keyboard shortcuts, press **Ctrl+C** in step 2 to issue the Copy command, and press **Ctrl+V** in step 5 to issue the Paste command.

✔ **The Windows Clipboard**
When you copy (or cut) a block of selected text, it gets placed on the *Windows Clipboard* (a storage area for text that is cut or copied). When you paste the text, Word copies it from the Clipboard into your document, leaving it on the Clipboard. If you want to paste it into several locations, just move the insertion point to each location and issue the Paste command again. The text is not removed from the Clipboard until you execute the next Copy or Cut command.

④ Move the insertion point to the place where you want to copy the text.

⑤ Click the **Paste** button on the Standard toolbar.

⑥ The text is copied to the new location.

End Task

# Task 7: Moving and Copying Multiple Items

## Using the Office Clipboard

In previous versions of Word, you can only move or copy one item (selection) at a time. Word 2000 removes this restriction with a new feature, the *Office Clipboard.* You "collect" multiple items of any length on the Office Clipboard (they can come from Word or any other Windows application), then paste them in any order into a Word document or any other Office document. This example shows you how to use the Copy command with the Office Clipboard to copy items, but you can also use the Cut command to move items.

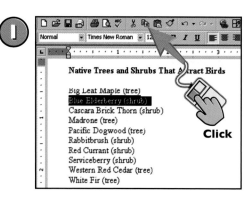

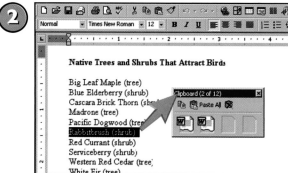

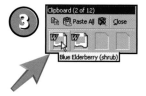

1. Select your first item and click the **Copy** button in the Standard toolbar. Then select and copy your second item.

2. As soon you copy (or cut) two items, the Clipboard toolbar appears with the Office Clipboard attached to it.

3. Word items are represented by Word icons. Hover over each one to display the beginning of the item in a ScreenTip.

4. If you like, add more items to the Office Clipboard (up to 12).

Next Step

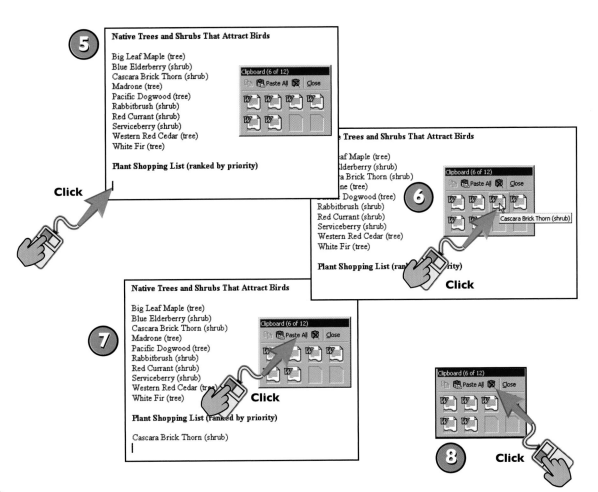

**Native Trees and Shrubs That Attract Birds**

Big Leaf Maple (tree)
Blue Elderberry (shrub)
Cascara Brick Thorn (shrub)
Madrone (tree)
Pacific Dogwood (tree)
Rabbitbrush (shrub)
Red Currant (shrub)
Serviceberry (shrub)
Western Red Cedar (tree)
White Fir (tree)

**Plant Shopping List (ranked by priority)**

Clipboard (6 of 12)
Paste All  Close

⑤ **Click**

Trees and Shrubs That Attract Birds

af Maple (tree)
lderberry (shrub)
a Brick Thorn (shrub)
ne (tree)
Dogwood (tree)
Rabbitbrush (shrub)
Red Currant (shrub)
Serviceberry (shrub)
Western Red Cedar (tree)
White Fir (tree)

**Plant Shopping List (ran    rity)**

Clipboard (6 of 12)
Paste All  Close

Cascara Brick Thorn (shrub)

⑥ **Click**

**Native Trees and Shrubs That Attract Birds**

Big Leaf Maple (tree)
Blue Elderberry (shrub)
Cascara Brick Thorn (shrub)
Madrone (tree)
Pacific Dogwood (tree)
Rabbitbrush (shrub)
Red Currant (shrub)
Serviceberry (shrub)
Western Red Cedar (tree)
White Fir (tree)

**Plant Shopping List (ranked by priority)**

Cascara Brick Thorn (shrub)

Clipboard (6 of 12)
Paste All  Close

⑦ **Click**

Clipboard (6 of 12)
Paste All  Close

⑧ **Click**

⑤ To insert an item, navigate to the document in which you want to paste the item and position the insertion point.

⑥ Click the item that you want to insert in the Office Clipboard.

⑦ The item is pasted into your document. (To paste all of the items in the Office Clipboard at once, click the **Paste All** toolbar button.)

⑧ To empty the Office Clipboard, click the **Clear Clipboard** button. To close the Clipboard toolbar, click the **Close** button.

**✓ Display the Clipboard toolbar**
**You don't have to wait until you've cut or copied two items to use the Clipboard toolbar. You can display it at any time by choosing View, Toolbars, Clipboard. When it's displayed, you can use the Copy button on the left end of the Clipboard toolbar or on the Standard toolbar; the two buttons do the same thing.**

End
Task

## Using Tabs

Word's *default tabs* are set every half inch across the page. When you press the Tab key, Word pushes the text to the right of the insertion point out to the next tab stop. The default tabs are all that you need if you just want to indent the first line of your paragraphs. If you want to use tabs to align text more precisely, however, you need to create *custom tabs* (see "Setting a Custom Left or Right Tab" in Part 6).

### ✓ What's a first-line indent?

Depending on how Word is set up on your computer, when you press the Tab key at the beginning of a paragraph, Word may actually set a *first-line indent* for the paragraph instead of inserting a tab. (See "Adding Indents" in Part 6.) The paragraph will look the same either way, and you can remove a first-line indent with the Backspace key.

# Task 8: Inserting a Tab

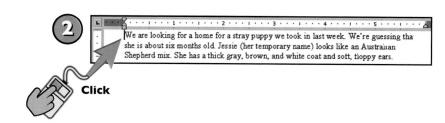

**Click**

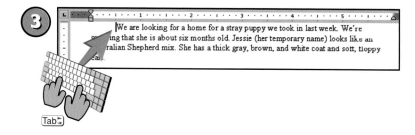

Tab

←Backspace

 The faint gray tickmarks spaced every half inch along the lower edge of the horizontal ruler represent Word's default tab stops.

 Move the insertion point to the location where you want to insert the tab.

 Press the **Tab** key. Word pushes the text out to the next default tab stop.

 To remove a tab, make sure that your insertion point is just to the right of the tab, and press the **Backspace** key.

End Task

# Task 9: Seeing Paragraph, Tab, and Space Marks

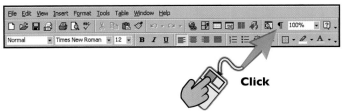

**Click**

> • We·are·looking·for·a·home·for·a·stray·puppy·we·took·in·last·week.·We're·guessing·that·she·is·about·six·months·old.·Jessie·(her·temporary·name)·looks·like·an·Australian·Shepherd·mix.·She·has·a·thick·gray,·brown,·and·white·coat·and·soft,·floppy·ears.¶

> • We·are·looking·for·a·home·for·a·stray·puppy·we·took·in·last·week.·We're·guessing·that·she·is·about·six·months·old.·Jessie·(her·temporary·name)·looks·like·an·Australian·Shepherd·mix.·She·has·a·thick·gray,·brown,·and·white·coat·and·soft,·floppy·ears.¶

(4)

> • We·are·looking·for·a·home·for·a·stray·puppy·we·took·in·last·week.·We're·guessing·that·she·is·about·six·months·old.·Jessie·(her·temporary·name)·looks·like·an·Australian·Shepherd·mix.·She·has·a·thick·gray,·brown,·and·white·coat·and·soft,·floppy·ears.¶

## Hiding and Displaying Hidden Symbols

The Show/Hide button is an extremely handy tool. It displays nonprinting symbols onscreen to show you where you pressed the Spacebar, the Enter key, and the Tab key. You might use this button to check whether you typed an extra space between two words, to see how many blank lines there are between two paragraphs, or to confirm that you inserted only one tab at the beginning of a paragraph.

(1) Click the **Show/Hide** button on the Standard toolbar.

(2) Word uses a dot to show where you pressed the Spacebar.

(3) Word uses an arrow to indicate where you pressed the Tab key.

(4) Word uses the **_paragraph mark_** symbol (¶) to indicate where you pressed Enter to end a paragraph.

 **A word about the Show/Hide button**
The Show/Hide button is a _toggle_ button. You click it once to turn it on, and again to turn it off. You can turn the Show/Hide button on and off whenever you choose.

Page
**61**

# Managing Word 2000 Documents

Just as a filing cabinet would be of no use if you weren't able to get files in to and out of the drawers, so you have to understand how to access and store Word documents on your computer system in order to use the program effectively. In this part, you learn elementary yet essential skills, including saving, closing, and opening documents, and creating new ones.

# Tasks

# Task 1: Saving a Document

## Saving a Document

A document you are typing exists only in your computer's *memory* until you save it. You must therefore save it to come back to your document later. After saving a document, you can continue working on it or close it.

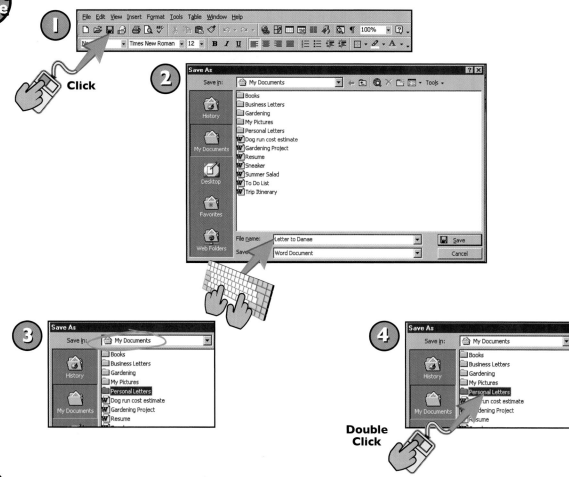

**Start Here**

**Click**

**Double Click**

✓ **Saving your document under a new name**
After you've saved a document for the first time, you still need to save every time you revise it. When you click the Save button these subsequent times, Word assumes you want to keep the same filename and location, so it saves immediately without displaying the Save As dialog box. To save the document with a different name or location, choose File, Save As instead.

① Click the **Save** button in the Standard toolbar to display the Save As dialog box.

② Type a name for the document in the **File name** text box. (You can include spaces.)

③ Look in the **Save in** box. If you want to save your file in the folder (or drive) listed here, skip to step 7.

④ If you want to save in a subfolder of the location in the **Save in** box, double-click the folder, and, if applicable, one of its subfolders.

Next Step

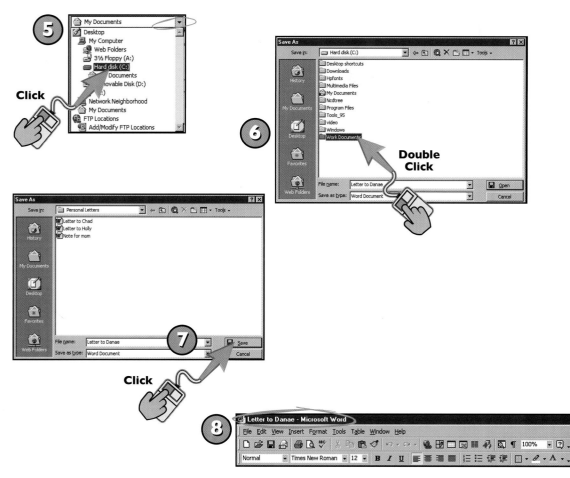

**5** Otherwise, click the **down arrow** to the right of the **Save in** box, and click the drive that contains the folder you want.

**6** Double-click folder names until the one you want is displayed in the **Save in** box.

**7** Click the **Save** button.

**8** The document's name now appears in the title bar of the Word window.

# Task 2: Closing a Document

## Closing a Document

When you are finished editing and saving a document, it's a good idea to close it. If you want to keep working on other documents, you can leave the Word window open. When you're ready to close Word itself, follow the steps in "Exiting Word 2000" in Part 1.

Start Here

Click

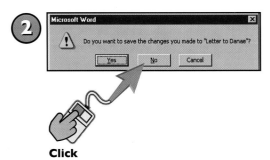

Click

Click

✓ **Another way to close your document**
If you like, you can choose File, Close in step 1 instead of clicking the Close button. The result is the same.

1. Click the **Close** button. (If you only have one Word window open, you will see two Close buttons. Click the lower one.) If you've saved all of your changes, Word closes the document immediately.

2. If you have unsaved changes, Word asks whether you want to save. If you don't, click the **No** button. Word closes the document.

3. If you want to save the changes you've made to the document, click the **Yes** button. (Click the **Cancel** button if you decide not to close the document after all.)

Next Step

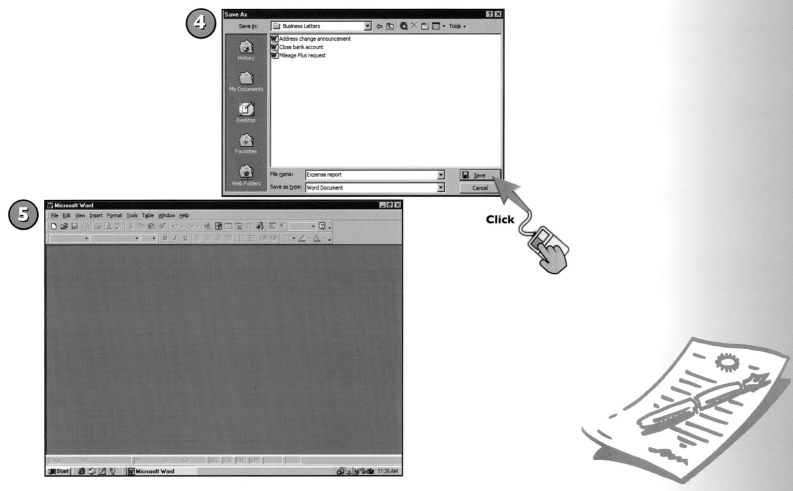

Click

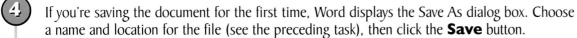

(4) If you're saving the document for the first time, Word displays the Save As dialog box. Choose a name and location for the file (see the preceding task), then click the **Save** button.

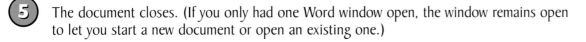

(5) The document closes. (If you only had one Word window open, the window remains open to let you start a new document or open an existing one.)

# Task 3: Opening a Document

## Opening a Document

When you want to revise a document that you've previously saved to disk, follow these steps to open it again. You can open as many documents at once as you like and use their taskbar buttons to switch back and forth between them.

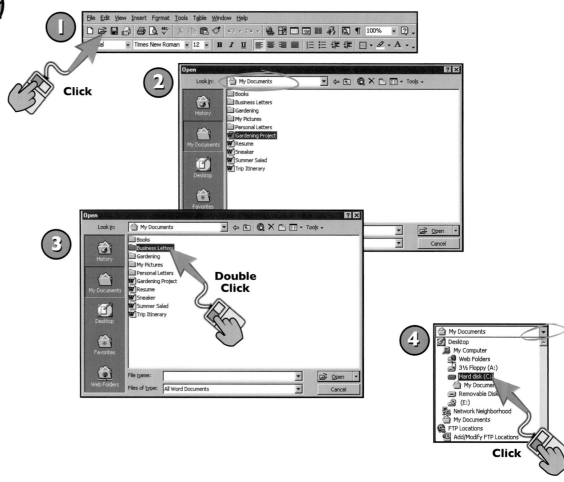

## Opening a document quickly

Word lists the four documents that you've opened most recently at the bottom of the File menu. If your document is in this list, you can just click it to open it instead of following these steps.

① Click the **Open** button in the Standard toolbar to display the Open dialog box.

② Look at the **Look in** box. If the folder (or drive) listed here is the one that contains your document, skip to step 6.

③ If the folder you want is a subfolder of the location in the **Look in** box, double-click the folder, and, if necessary, one of its subfolders.

④ Otherwise, click the **down arrow** to the right of the **Look in** list. Click the drive that contains the folder and document you want.

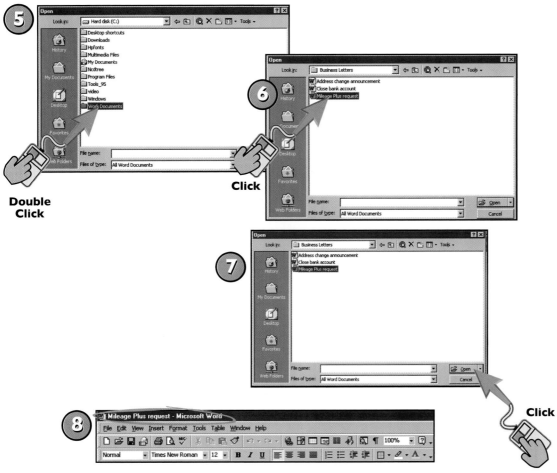

Double
Click

Click

Click

**5** Double-click folder names until the folder that contains your document is displayed in the **Look in** box.

**6** Click the document name.

**7** Click the **Open** button. (You can also just double-click the document name.)

**8** Word opens the document for you.

# Task 4: Getting to Your Favorite Folders and Documents

## Accessing Frequently Used Folders and Documents

If a folder or document you use frequently is buried deep in the folder structure on your hard disk or is off on another network computer, it can be time-consuming to navigate to it in the Open and Save As dialog boxes. Fortunately, you can avoid this hassle by creating a *shortcut* to the folder or document in your Favorites folder. The shortcut simply points to the folder or document. Clicking it opens the folder or document just as if you clicked the item itself.

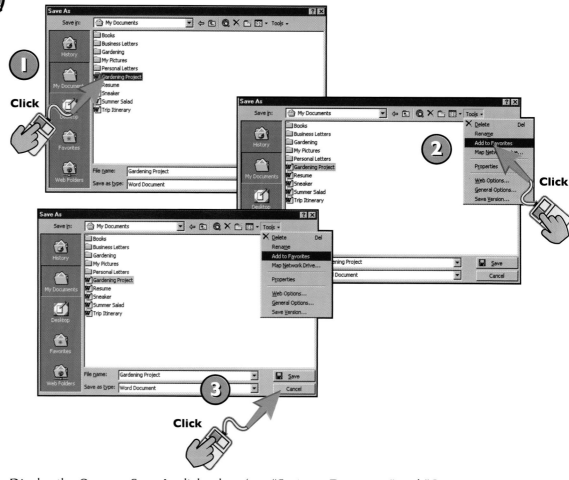

**Start Here**

Click

Click

Click

**1** Display the Open or Save As dialog box (see "Saving a Document" and "Opening a Document" earlier in Part 4), and select the item you want to create a shortcut for.

**2** Choose **Tools**, **Add to Favorites** at the top of the dialog box.

**3** Repeat steps 1 and 2 to add other shortcuts to your Favorites folder if you like, then click the **Cancel** button.

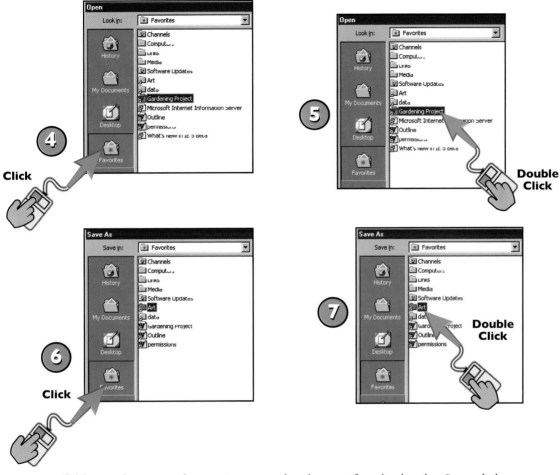

**Click**

**Double Click**

**Click**

**Double Click**

4️⃣ To open a folder or document that you've created a shortcut for, display the Open dialog box, and click the **Favorites** folder in the *Places Bar*.

5️⃣ Double-click the desired shortcut in the Favorites folder.

6️⃣ To save a document to a folder for which you created a shortcut, display the Save As dialog box, and click the **Favorites** folder in the Places Bar.

7️⃣ Double-click the shortcut for the folder, then continue with the save process.

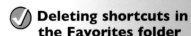

✅ **Deleting shortcuts in the Favorites folder**
To delete a shortcut to a favorite folder or document, right-click the shortcut and click Delete. Deleting a shortcut does not remove the document or folder to which the shortcut pointed.

## Creating a New Document

Each time you start Word 2000, you get a new blank document that has the temporary name Document1 (which you replace the first time you save). However, you may at times want to start a second or third document in the same Word session. Word lets you keep multiple documents open at once, each in its own Word window, so you don't have to close the currently active document before beginning another one.

# Task 5: Creating a New Document

Start Here

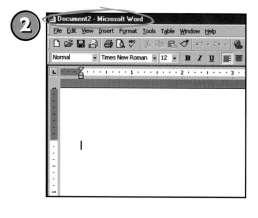

Click

Click

(1) Click the **New Blank Document** button in the Standard toolbar.

(2) A Word window opens with a new blank document.

(3) This time, choose **File**, **New** instead of clicking the New Blank Document button to display the New dialog box.

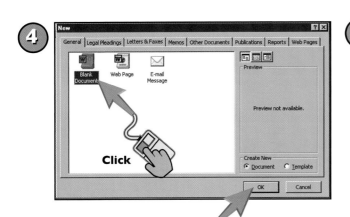

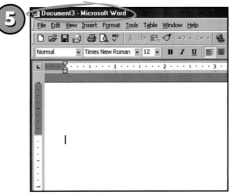

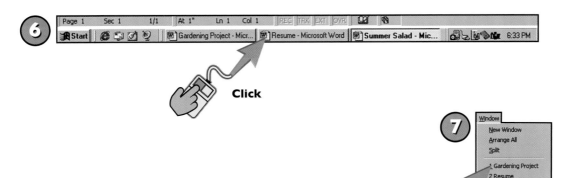

**(4)** Click the **General** tab and select the **Blank Document** icon, and click the **OK** button.

**(5)** Word displays a new document, just as if you had clicked the New Blank Document button. (See the next task to find out when the File, New command is useful.)

**(6)** To switch among open documents, click the taskbar button for the desired document.

**(7)** You can also switch among open documents by clicking the Window menu in any open Word window, then clicking the desired document at the bottom of the menu.

✓ **New document names**
When you start a new document, its name may be Document2, Document3, and so on. The number in the name does not mean that you have that number of documents currently *open*. It just means that you *started* that many documents in the current Word session.

End Task

# Task 6: Standardizing the Look of Your Documents

## Using a Template

You can type and format all of your documents from scratch, but you don't have to. Word's *templates* can help you create a variety of documents, from memos and letters to fax cover sheets. A template is a rough blueprint for a document that usually includes some combination of text and formatting. When you use the **New Blank Document** toolbar button to start a document, Word assumes you want to use the **Normal** template, which starts you off with a "plain vanilla" document. Here you learn to use other templates containing text and more complex formatting.

**Click**

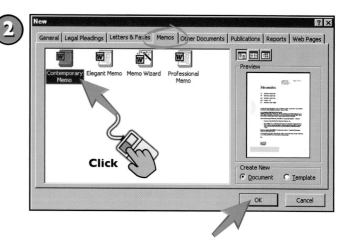

**Click**

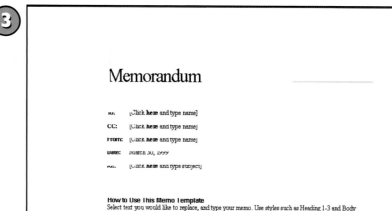

Memorandum

To: [Click here and type name]

CC: [Click here and type name]

From: [Click here and type name]

Date: March 30, 1999

Re: [Click here and type subject]

How to Use This Memo Template
Select text you would like to replace, and type your memo. Use styles such as Heading 1-3 and Body text in the Style control on the Formatting toolbar.

**1** Choose **File**, **New** to display the New dialog box.

**2** Click the tab that contains the template you want to use (your tabs may differ from the ones shown here), select the template, and click the **OK** button.

**3** Word creates a new document based on the template.

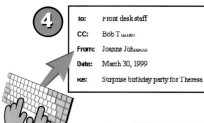

| | |
|---|---|
| **To:** | Front desk staff |
| **CC:** | Bob Turner |
| **From:** | Joanne Johnson |
| **Date:** | March 30, 1999 |
| **Re:** | Surprise birthday party for Theresa |

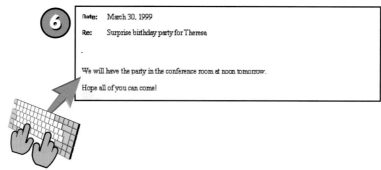

**Date:** March 30, 1999

**Re:** Surprise birthday party for Therese

**How to Use This Memo Template**
Select text you would like to replace, and type your memo. Use styles such as Heading 1-3 and Body Text in the Style control on the Formatting toolbar.

To delete the background elements—such as the circle, rectangles, or return address frames, click on the boundary border to highlight the "handles," and press Delete. To replace the picture in this template with a different one, first click on the picture. Then, on the Insert menu, point to Picture, and click From File. Locate the folder that contains the picture you want to insert, then double-click the picture.

To save changes to this template for future use, choose Save As from the File menu. In the Save As Type box, choose Document Template. Next time you want to use it, choose New from the File menu, and then double-click your template.

**Date:** March 30, 1999

**Re:** Surprise birthday party for Theresa

.

We will have the party in the conference room at noon tomorrow.

Hope all of you can come!

---

**4** Click the **Click Here and Type** instructions, and type over them with the text you want in your document.

**5** Some templates have instructions on using the template where the body of the document will go. If yours does, first read the information.

**6** Then select the information, and type over it with your text. (Your text replaces the selected instructions.) Optionally save, and then close the document.

**✓ Saving templates**
When you save a document that you based on a template, Word saves it separately from the template. The template maintains its original appearance so that you can use it over and over again.

# Task 7: Using a Wizard to Create Your Document

## Using a Wizard

If you'd appreciate a bit more handholding than you get with standard templates, try using a *Wizard*. Wizards, like other templates, give you "blueprint" text and formatting. But they also ask you questions about what you want to include in the document and create just what you asked for. Wizard-generated documents look exactly like documents based on standard templates, complete with "click here" instructions to help you fill in the text.

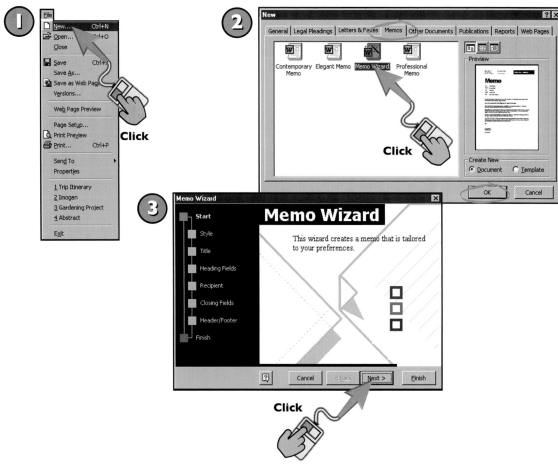

Choose **File**, **New** to display the New dialog box.

Click the **Memos** tab, select the **Memo Wizard** template, and click **OK** to start the Wizard.

Word displays the first "page" of the Wizard. Click the **Next** button.

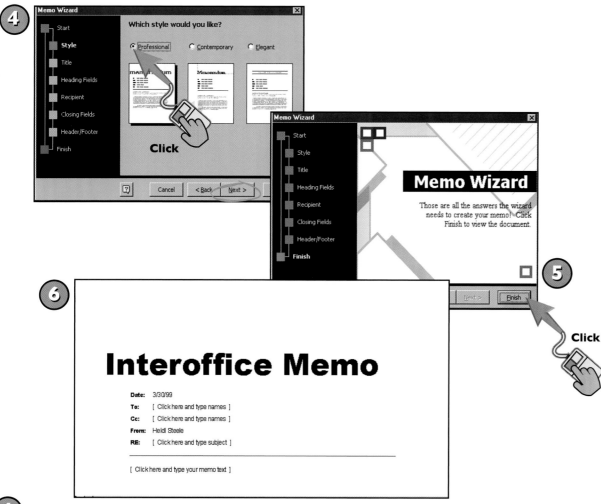

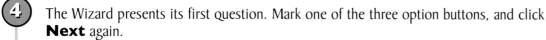

④ The Wizard presents its first question. Mark one of the three option buttons, and click **Next** again.

⑤ Continue answering the Wizard's questions, clicking Next to progress from one dialog box to the next. When you reach the last one, click the **Finish** button.

⑥ In a moment, the document appears. Close it without saving it.

# Task 8: Finding a Document

## Finding a Document

If you have trouble finding a document that you know you saved, you can use Word's Find feature to search for it. This feature is especially useful if you can't remember what you named the document, because you can search for a word or phrase contained within the document. The Find command is accessible from the Open dialog box, so it's right there when you need it.

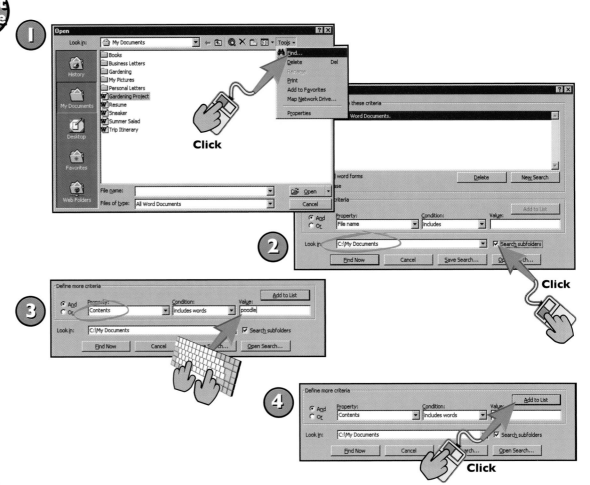

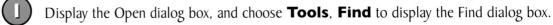

**Click**

**Click**

**Click**

① Display the Open dialog box, and choose **Tools**, **Find** to display the Find dialog box.

② Display the folder that you want to search in the **Look In** box. If you think your document might be in a subfolder of this folder, mark the **Search Subfolders** check box.

③ Choose **Contents** in the **Property** drop-down list to search for the document by looking for a particular word or phrase it contains. Then type the word or phrase in the **Value** text box.

④ Click the **Add to List** button.

Next Step

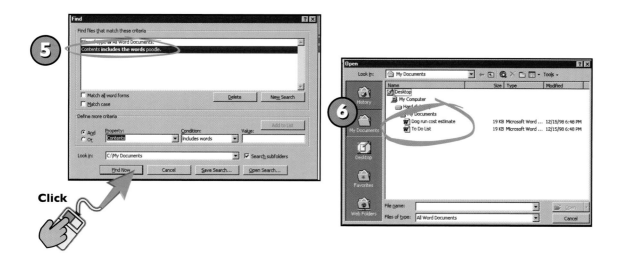

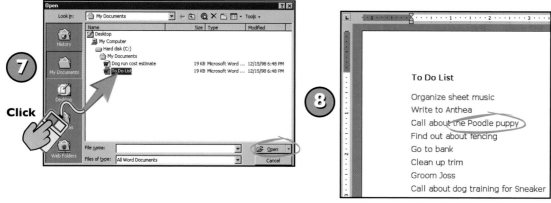

**5** The search criteria you specified is now included in the list at the top of the dialog box. Click the **Find Now** button to begin the search.

**6** In a moment, Word displays a list of the files that contain your text, and it shows you where each one is stored.

**7** To open one of the files, select it and click the **Open** button. (You can also just double-click the file.)

**8** Word opens the document for you.

# Viewing and Printing the Document

You can create such a wide variety of documents in Word (from standard letters, memos, and reports to sophisticated flyers and newsletters) that Word gives you a broad set of choices for viewing documents onscreen and printing them. The first three tasks in this part discuss viewing options; the last three teach you basic printing techniques.

# Tasks

# Task 1: Changing Views

## Using Print Layout and Normal View

Word provides several different *views* that you can use to work with your documents. **Print Layout** view, the default, shows the margin areas of your document, so you can see margin elements, such as page numbers and headers and footers. You need to use **Print Layout** view to work with columns and graphics, among other things. If you are typing a document that doesn't contain a lot of formatting, Normal view should work well for you. This view doesn't show your margin areas, but it gives you a simple uncluttered view of your text.

✓ **Changing Views**
If you like, you can switch views by clicking one of the four View buttons in the lower-left corner of the Word window, directly to the left of the horizontal scroll bar.

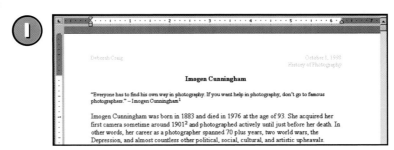
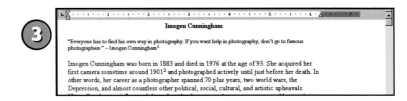
**Click**

**Click**

1 Print Layout view gives you vertical and horizontal rulers. The margin areas are visible, and you can see the edge of the page. (The area off the edge of the page is dark gray.)

2 Choose **View**, **Normal** to switch to Normal view.

3 In Normal view, you can't see the margin areas, and you don't have a vertical ruler.

4 Choose **View**, **Print Layout** to switch back to Print Layout view.

# Task 2: Zooming a Document

**Start Here**

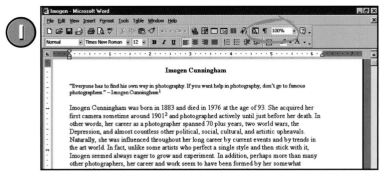

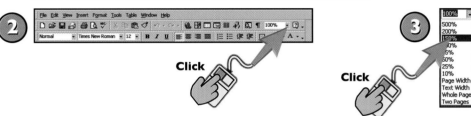

**Click**

**Click**

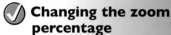

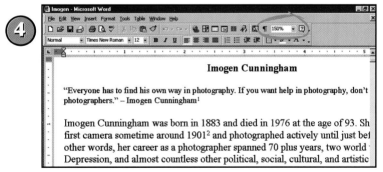

## Zooming a Document

Depending on the resolution of your monitor and the size of your text, there may be times when you want to *zoom* in on your text to enlarge it so that you can get a better look at your text, or zoom out to shrink it to see more of the page. Zooming doesn't affect the size of the text when it prints; it only affects its appearance on your screen.

✓ **Changing the zoom percentage**
If the zoom setting you want (85%, perhaps) isn't one of the options in the Zoom list, just click the current entry in the Zoom box to select it, type a new number (you don't need to type the percent sign), and press Enter.

✓ **Using other zoom settings**
The end of the Zoom list contains four handy options for zooming to the width of your page, the width of your text, the entire page, and two pages. Feel free to try these settings.

**(1)** Note the setting in the Zoom box at the right end of the Standard toolbar. By default, Word displays documents at 100% magnification.

**(2)** Click the **down arrow** to the right of the Zoom box.

**(3)** Click the magnification percentage you want to use.

**(4)** Word applies the setting you chose.

**End Task**

Page
**83**

# Task 3: Previewing a Document

## Using Print Preview

Word enables you to see what the printed document will look like before you actually send it to the printer. Using Print Preview is a great way to avoid wasting paper because you can spot problems in your document before you print.

**Start Here**

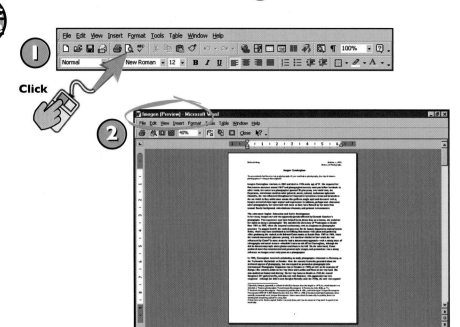

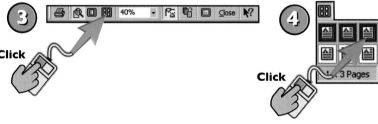

⊘ **Fit your document on one page**

If your document is spilling over onto two pages and you'd like to get it to fit on one page, you can click the **Shrink to Fit** button on the Print Preview toolbar (the fourth button from the right) to make the text fit on a single page.

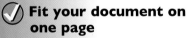

① Click the **Print Preview** button in the Standard toolbar.

② Word switches to Print Preview. (The title bar now contains **Preview**.) Press the **Page Up** and **Page Down** keys to bring different parts of the document into view.

③ To view several pages at the same time, click the **Multiple Pages** button.

④ Drag through the number of pages you want to view in the grid that drops down.

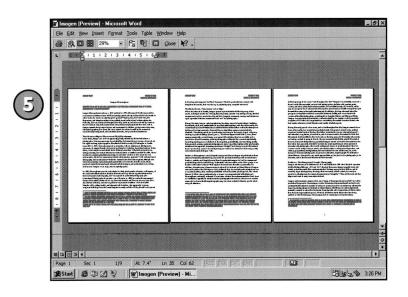

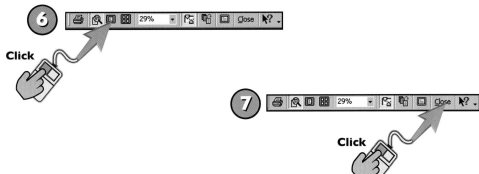

**Click**

**Click**

**5** Word displays the number of pages you selected.

**6** To return to viewing one page, click the **One Page** button.

**7** To close Print Preview, click the **Close** button.

End Task

## Printing a Document

Word assumes that you will frequently want to print one complete copy of your document, so it provides a toolbar button to let you do just that. If you need to customize your printing at all, you'll find all the options you need in the Print dialog box. Before you follow these steps, make sure that your printer is turned on.

# Task 4: Printing a Document

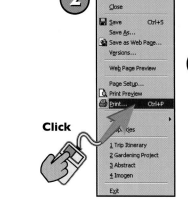

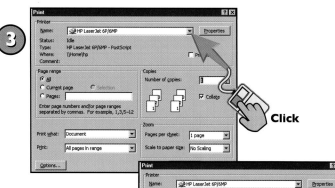

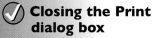

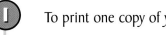

✓ **Closing the Print dialog box**

If you display the Print dialog box but then decide you are not ready to print yet, be sure to click the **Cancel** button instead of the **OK** button to close the dialog box without printing.

 To print one copy of your document, click the **Print** button on the Standard toolbar.

 For other printing options, choose **File**, **Print** to display the Print dialog box.

 If you have more than one printer, select the one you want in the **Name** drop-down list.

④ To print only the page that the insertion point is on, click the **Current page** option button.

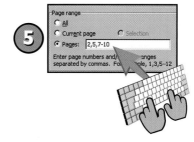

**5**

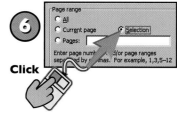

**Click**

**6**

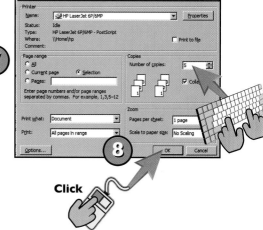

**7**

**8**

**Click**

 **5** To print a range of pages, type the page numbers in the **Pages** text box. In this example, Word will print pages 2, 5, 7, 8, 9, and 10.

 **6** To print only a block of text, select the text before displaying the Print dialog box, and then mark the **Selection** option button.

 **7** To print multiple copies, type the number in the **Number of copies** text box.

 **8** When you've made your choices, click the **OK** button.

✓ **Print multiple pages on one sheet of paper**
Word 2000 can scale your document pages much like a high-end copy machine can. To print more than one document page on a sheet of paper, choose the number of pages in the **Pages per sheet** drop-down list in the Print dialog box.

# Task 5: Printing an Envelope

## Printing an Envelope

Printing an envelope in Word is simple. You check to make sure that the address is right, put the envelope in the printer, and issue the command to print. Word assumes you want to print on a standard business-size envelope, but you can choose a different envelope size if necessary.

**Start Here**

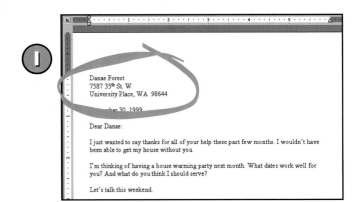

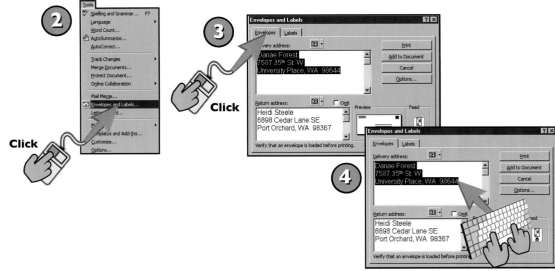

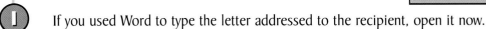

✓ **Delivery address**
You can follow the steps here even if you don't have a document that contains the recipient's address on-screen. You just have to take the extra step of typing the delivery address in step 4.

**1** If you used Word to type the letter addressed to the recipient, open it now.

**2** Choose **Tools**, **Envelopes and Labels**.

**3** Click the **Envelopes** tab in the Envelopes and Labels dialog box.

**4** Word finds the address in the document you have open onscreen. Edit it in the **Delivery Address** box if needed.

Next Step

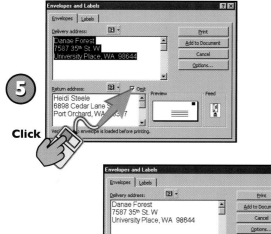

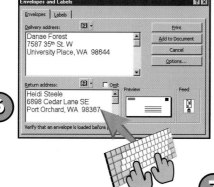

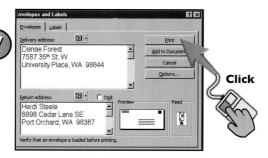

**Click**

Word automatically includes your return address on the envelope. If you have envelopes with a preprinted return address, mark the **Omit** check box.

If you want to print a return address, check the address in the **Return address** box and edit it if necessary.

Put the envelope in your printer and click the **Print** button. If you edited your return address in the previous step, Word will ask whether you want to make the address you typed the default return address for future documents. Click **Yes** if you do.

✅ **Feeding the envelope.**
If you aren't sure how to insert your envelope into your printer, look at the Feed area in the Envelopes and Labels dialog box. It shows the correct orientation for your envelope in your printer. Beware though; this feature is not always correct. If you try the Feed area's suggested orientation and the envelope comes out wrong, consult your printer documentation.

✅ **Your return address**
Word stores your return address in the User Information tab of the Options dialog box (Tools, Options) and uses it in a variety of situations. You can change it here at any time.

End Task

# Printing Labels

The steps for printing labels are very similar to those described in the previous task for printing envelopes. The one difference is that you'll probably need to choose another label type because labels come in such a wide variety of sizes.

**(!) Printing sheets of labels**
Even though Word allows you to print a single label at a time (see step 7), it is not a good idea to run a sheet of labels through a laser printer more than once. Doing so can cause labels to come off inside the printer, something that is not cheap to repair.

# Task 6: Printing Labels

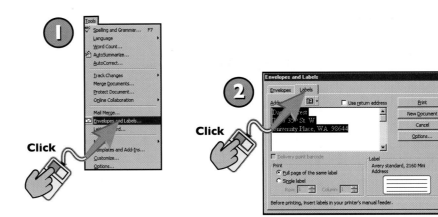

Click

Click

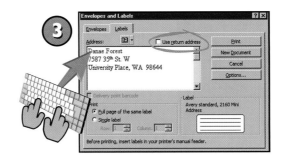

Click

**1** Choose **Tools**, **Envelopes and Labels**.

**2** Click the **Labels** tab.

**3** Type (or edit) the address in the **Address** box. If you want to print your return address instead, mark the **Use return address** check box.

**4** Click the **Options** button to display the Label Options dialog box.

Next Step

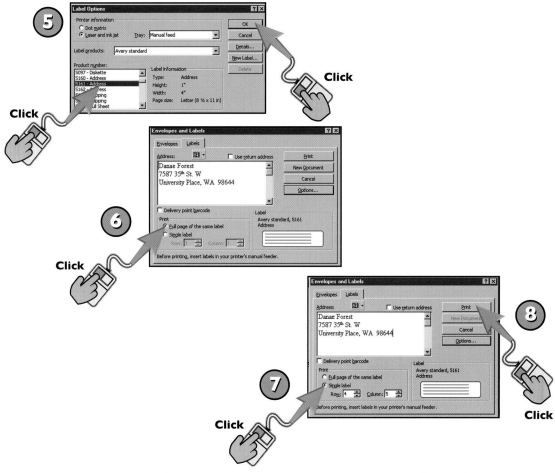

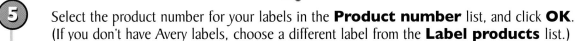

**5** Select the product number for your labels in the **Product number** list, and click **OK**. (If you don't have Avery labels, choose a different label from the **Label products** list.)

**6** Click the **Full page of the same label** option button if you want a whole page of labels with the same address on each one.

**7** If you want a single label, mark the **Single label** option button, and then enter the label's row and column number.

**8** Put the sheet of labels in your printer, and click the **Print** button.

# Formatting Characters and Paragraphs

Formatting a document (improving its appearance) can be a lot of fun, but it can also leave you rather befuddled if you don't understand how the formatting commands work. This part gives you an organized introduction to the techniques you'll use every day to format characters and paragraphs. You start with changing fonts and font size, applying bold, italic, underline, and so on. You also learn formatting that affects paragraphs, such as setting alignment, adding indents, and working with custom tabs.

# Tasks

## Adding Emphasis to Text

Applying a little **bold**, *italics*, or <u>underlining</u> here and there can add just the right emphasis to your document. You can also apply more than one of these three formats to the same text. A word that has all three formats applied looks like <u>***this***</u>.

**Applying formatting first.**

If you've already typed your text, you must select it before applying bold, italic, or underline. If you haven't typed it yet, you can click where the text will begin, turn on the formatting option, and then start typing. The text you type takes on the formatting you've applied. This works for all other font and paragraph formatting commands as well.

# Task 1: Making Text Bold, Italic, and Underlined

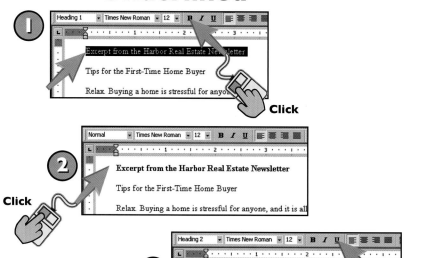

**1** To make text bold, select the text and click the **Bold** button on the Formatting toolbar.

**2** Click anywhere to deselect the text so that you can see the bold formatting more easily.

**3** To underline text, select the text and click the **Underline** button on the Formatting toolbar.

**4** Click anywhere to deselect the text so that you can see the underlining more clearly.

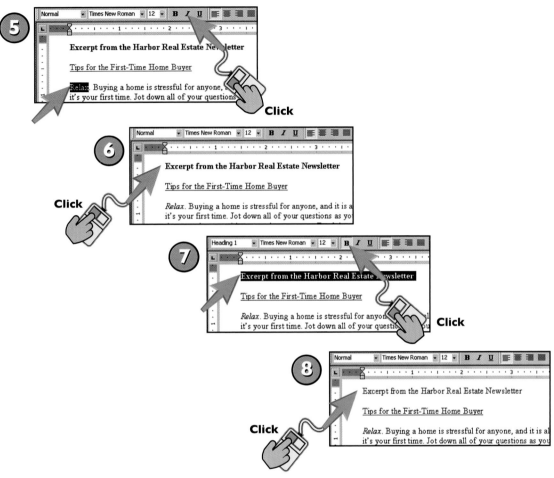

**5** To italicize text, select the text and click the **Italic** button on the Formatting toolbar.

**6** Click anywhere to deselect the text so that you can view the italicized characters.

**7** To turn off bold, italic, or underlining, select the text first, then click the appropriate button. (In this example, bold is turned on.)

**8** Click anywhere to deselect the text. You can now see that the formatting is turned off.

**Shortcut keys**
Instead of clicking the Bold, Italic, and Underline toolbar buttons, you can also press **Ctrl+B** for bold, **Ctrl+I** for italic, and **Ctrl+U** for underlining.

# Task 2: Changing the Font and Font Size

## Changing the Font and Font Size

One of the things people like most about word processing is the ability to quickly change the *font* (typeface) and font size of your text. Font size is measured in *points*. (A 10-point to 12-point font is commonly used for body text.) Word assumes that you want to use a Times New Roman, 12-point font, but as you'll see here, you can change these settings with just a couple of mouse clicks.

✓ **Frequently used fonts**
The fonts that you use the most frequently appear above the horizontal double line in the Font list so that you can get to them easily (see the figure for step 3). Below the double line is an alpha-betical list of all your fonts.

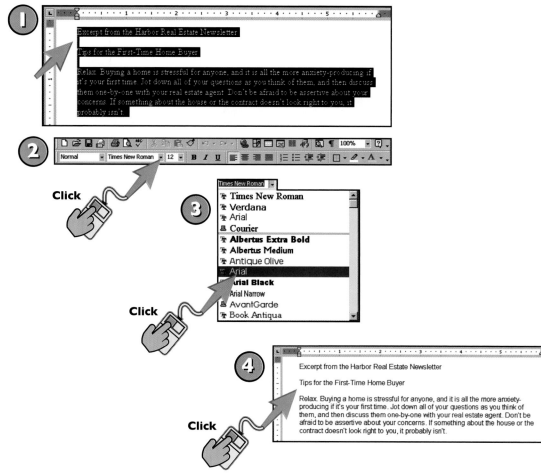

Start Here

Click

Click

Click

1. Select the text you want to change.

2. Click the **down arrow** to the right of the **Font** list in the Formatting toolbar.

3. Use the scroll bar on the right edge of the list to move through the list, and click the font that you want to use. Notice that the font names show you what each font will look like.

4. Click anywhere to deselect the text so that you can see the new font more clearly.

Next Step

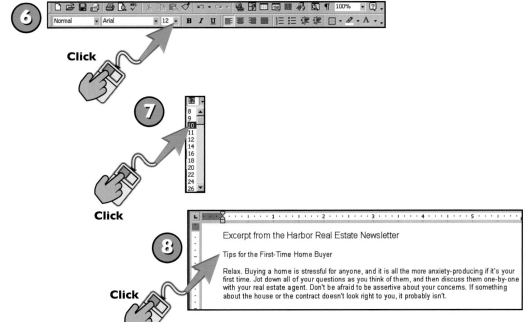

**Click**

**Click**

**Click**

(5) Select the text you want to change.

(6) Click the **down arrow** to the right of the **Font Size** list in the Formatting toolbar.

(7) Scroll through the list, and click the size that you want to use.

(8) Click anywhere to deselect the text so that you can more easily see the new size.

**✓ Choosing types of fonts**

The symbols to the left of the font names in the Font list tell you about the font (see the figure for step 3). The TT symbol indicates a *TrueType* font. These fonts are easy to use because they look the same onscreen as they do when printed. The printer icon indicates a *printer font*. Printer fonts will look great when printed, but their onscreen appearance may not exactly match the printed version.

# Task 3: Adding Highlighting and Color to Your Text

Start Here

## Highlighting and Coloring Text

Word offers a highlight feature you can use just as you would a highlighter pen. This tool comes in handy when you're editing text onscreen—it enables you to call attention to blocks of text you want to comment on, that need further revision, and so on. Word also lets you change the color of characters themselves (not the background behind the characters) by applying a font color. Although highlighting is useful regardless of whether you have a color printer (if you don't have a color printer, the highlighting will print in a shade of gray), you're not as likely to use font colors unless you can print in color.

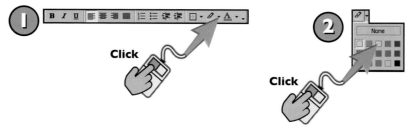

Click

Click

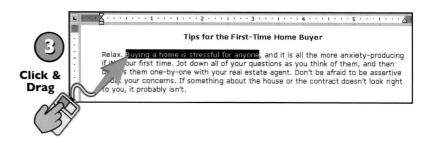

Click & Drag

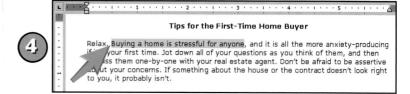

(1) Click the **down arrow** to the right of the **Highlight** button on the Formatting toolbar.

(2) Click the color that you want to use in the palette that appears.

(3) The mouse pointer takes on the shape of a highlighter pen. Drag across the text, and then release the mouse button.

(4) The text is now highlighted with the color you chose.

Next Step ▶

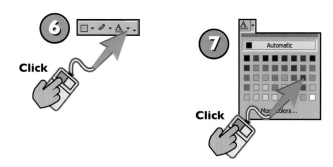

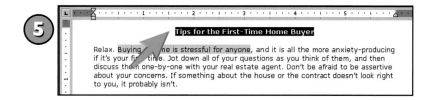

**Click**

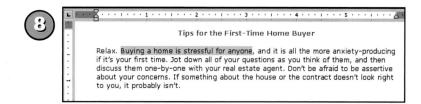

**Click**

(5) To change your font color, start by selecting the text.

(6) Click the **down arrow** to the right of the **Font Color** button on the Formatting toolbar.

(7) Click the desired color in the palette that appears.

(8) Click anywhere to deselect your text and see the font color that you applied.

**Remove highlighting and font color**
To remove highlighting, select the text, click the **down arrow** to the right of the **Highlight** button in the Formatting toolbar, and then choose **None.** To remove font color, select the text, click the **down arrow** to the right of the **Font Color** button in the Formatting toolbar, and then choose **Automatic.**

End Task

# Task 4: Changing Paragraph Alignment

## Changing Paragraph Alignment

*Alignment* refers to the way the right and left edges of a paragraph line up along the margins. By default, Word uses left alignment, which gives paragraphs a straight left edge and a ragged right edge. You usually use centering and right alignment for headings or other short lines of text. Occasionally, you may want to *justify* paragraphs so that both the right and left edges are straight. Justified text is frequently used in magazines and newspapers. To change alignment, you use the four alignment buttons on the Formatting toolbar.

**Click**

**Click**

① The paragraph that contains the insertion point is left-aligned, so the **Align Left** button looks like it's pushed in.

② To center a paragraph, select it and click the **Center** button.

③ Click anywhere to deselect the paragraph.

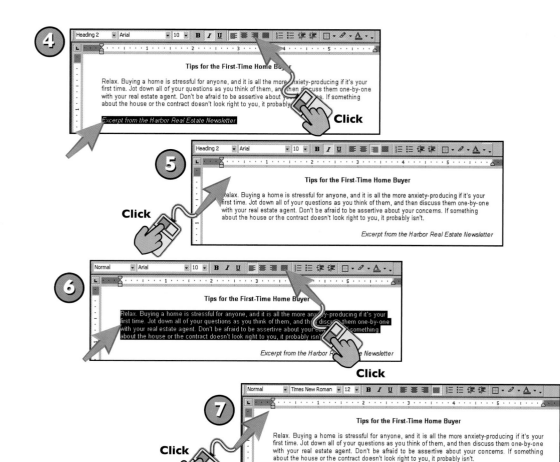

**4** To right-align a paragraph, select it and click the **Align Right** button.

**5** Click anywhere to deselect the paragraph.

**6** To justify a paragraph, select it and click the **Justify** button.

**7** Click anywhere to deselect the paragraph.

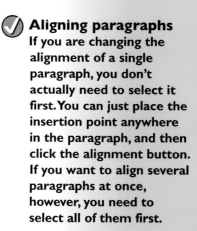

✓ **Aligning paragraphs**
If you are changing the alignment of a single paragraph, you don't actually need to select it first. You can just place the insertion point anywhere in the paragraph, and then click the alignment button. If you want to align several paragraphs at once, however, you need to select all of them first.

# Task 5: Changing Line Spacing

## Changing Line Spacing

*Line spacing* is the amount of space between lines within a paragraph. Word assumes single spacing, but you can change this setting to double spacing, which is great for rough drafts (you have room to write your edits between the lines), or one-and-a-half line spacing, which can make your text easier to read.

Start Here

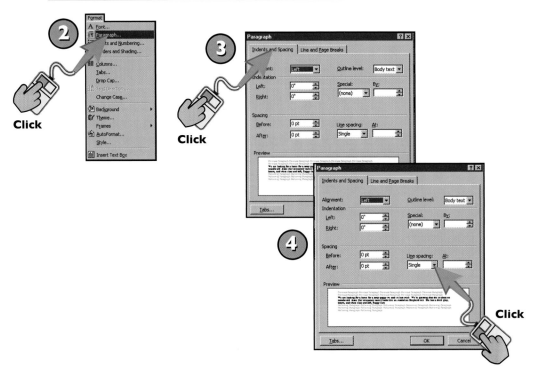

Click    Click    Click

✓ **Use the keyboard to change line spacing**
If you don't like the hassle of displaying the Paragraph dialog box, you can change line spacing with the keyboard instead. **Select the paragraphs and then press Ctrl+2 for double spacing, Ctrl+5 for one-and-a-half line spacing, or Ctrl+1 for single spacing.**

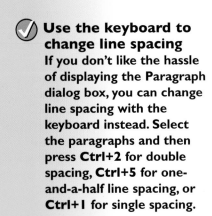

① Select the paragraphs you want to change.

② Choose **Format, Paragraph** to display the Paragraph dialog box.

③ Click the **Indents and Spacing** tab if it isn't already in front.

④ Click the **down arrow** to the right of the **Line spacing** list.

Next Step

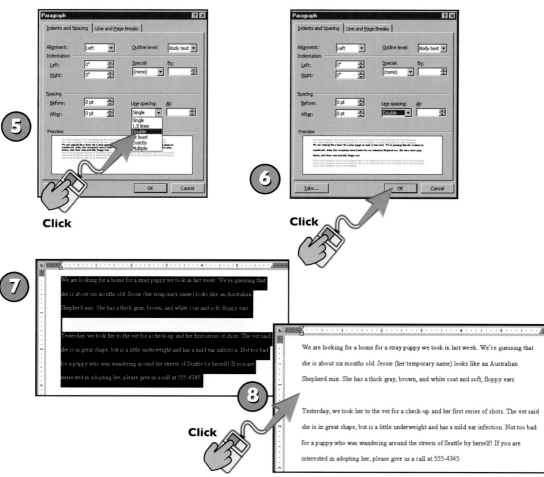

**5** Click the desired spacing in the list.

**6** Click the **OK** button.

**7** Word applies the line spacing you chose to the selected paragraphs.

**8** Click anywhere to deselect the text.

✓ **Repeating your last action.**
You can press F4 to repeat your last action. While this shortcut works for all almost all actions, it is especially useful for formatting. If you have just applied formatting that required going into a dialog box and now want to apply the same formatting elsewhere, just select the desired block of text and press F4.

End Task

# Task 6: Adding Indents

## Indenting Paragraphs

Word enables you to indent paragraphs from the left margin, the right margin, or both. You can also create a first-line indent, which indents only the first line of a paragraph, or a hanging indent, which indents all of the lines except the first. Word provides several ways to set indents. Here, you learn to add indents by dragging the indent markers on the ruler. To undo any indent you set, select the indented paragraphs and then drag the appropriate marker back to its original position on the ruler.

Click & Drag

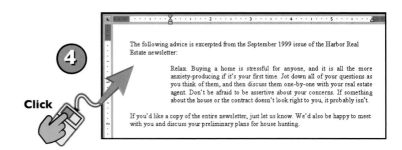

Click

**1** To set a left indent, first select the paragraph you want to indent.

**2** Point to the **Left Indent** marker (the square underneath the two triangles). The ScreenTip *Left Indent* appears.

**3** Drag the **Left Indent** marker to the desired position on the ruler. As you drag, the text is indented. When it's in the right place, release the mouse button.

**4** Click anywhere to deselect the text.

Next Step

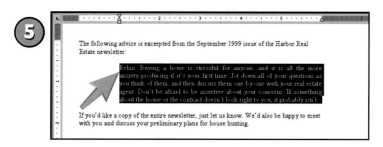

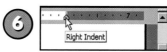

Click & Drag

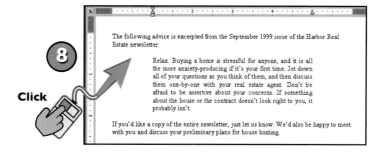

Click

**5** To set a right indent, first select the paragraphs you want to indent.

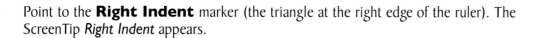

**6** Point to the **Right Indent** marker (the triangle at the right edge of the ruler). The ScreenTip *Right Indent* appears.

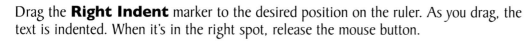

**7** Drag the **Right Indent** marker to the desired position on the ruler. As you drag, the text is indented. When it's in the right spot, release the mouse button.

**8** Click anywhere to deselect the text.

**First-line and hanging indents**
To create a first-line indent, select the paragraphs and then drag the **First Line Indent** marker (the top triangle above the Left Indent marker). To create a hanging indent, select the paragraphs and drag the **Hanging Indent** marker (the bottom triangle directly above the Left Indent marker).

End Task

## Bulleted and Numbered Lists

Setting off items in a list with numbers or bullets is a great way to present information clearly. Word's bulleted and numbered list features add the bullets or numbers for you, and they even create hanging indents so that when text in an item wraps to the next line, it doesn't wrap underneath the number or bullet.

# Task 7: Creating Bulleted and Numbered Lists

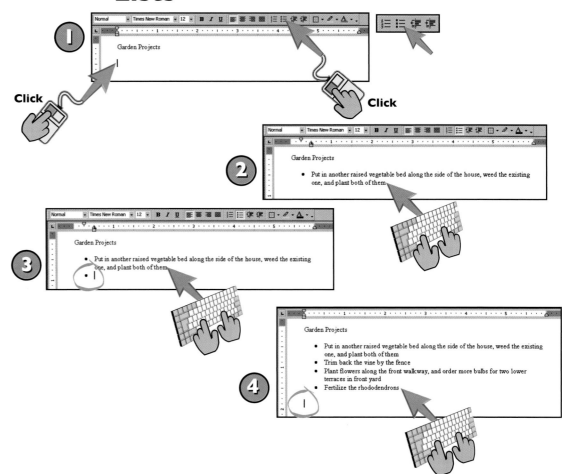

**Click**

**Click**

✓ **Creating blank lines between items**
If you want a blank line in between items in a bulleted or numbered list, press **Shift+Enter** and then **Enter** at the end of each item (instead of just pressing **Enter**).

① Click where you want the list to start, and then click the **Bullets** button on the Formatting toolbar.

② Word inserts a bullet. Type the first item in the list.

③ Press Enter. Word inserts a bullet on the next line for you.

④ Continue typing items in your list. After the last item, press Enter twice to turn off the bullets.

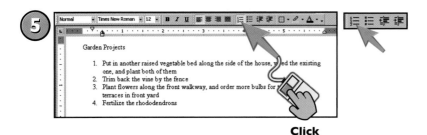

**Click**

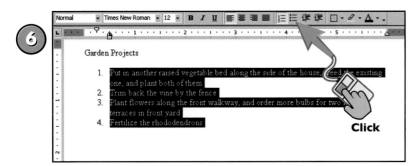

**Click**

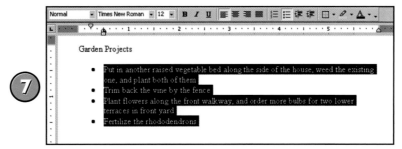

⑤ To create a numbered list, follow steps 1 through 4, but click the **Numbering** button on the Formatting toolbar in step 1 instead.

⑥ To switch from numbers to bullets (or vice versa), select the list, and then click the **Bullets** or **Numbering** button.

⑦ Word makes the change for you. Click anywhere to deselect the text.

✓ **Automatic renumbering**
One of the advantages of using Word's numbered list feature is that when you add, delete, or move items in a list, Word keeps the numbering sequential.

✓ **Turning off the automatic bullets and numbering**
You may notice that Word automatically turns on the bulleted or numbered list feature as soon as you type a line beginning with an asterisk (*) or a number and press **Enter**. If you like this feature, great. If you don't, you can turn it off: Choose **Tools, AutoCorrect,** click the **AutoFormat As You Type** tab, clear the check boxes for **Automatic bulleted lists** and **Automatic numbered lists,** and click **OK.**

## Setting a Custom Left or Right Tab

Word's default tab stops are fine for many documents (see "Inserting a Tab" in Part 3). But in some situations, you need to specify the exact type and position of your tab stops. Word provides five types of custom tabs: left (the default tabs are also left tabs), right, center, decimal, and bar. You learn about left and right tabs here, and about center and decimal tabs in the next task.

# Task 8: Setting a Custom Left or Right Tab

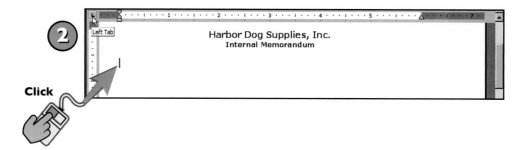
Click

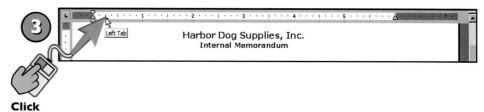
Click

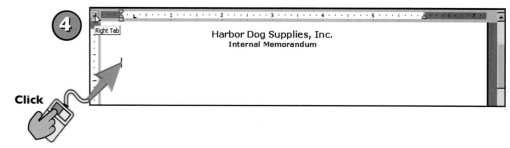
Click

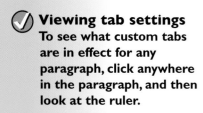
**Viewing tab settings**
To see what custom tabs are in effect for any paragraph, click anywhere in the paragraph, and then look at the ruler.

1. Before you insert any type of custom tab, first click the **Tab Stop Indicator** button until you see the symbol for the tab you want.

2. To insert a left tab, display the left-tab symbol on the **Tab Stop Indicator** button, and click in the paragraph where you want to use the tab.

3. Click at the desired location on the ruler to insert the tab.

4. To insert a right tab, display the right-tab symbol on the **Tab Stop Indicator** button, and click in the paragraph where you want to use the tab.

Next Step

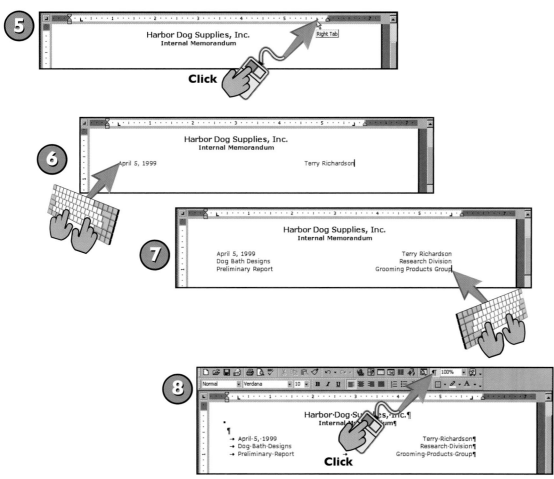

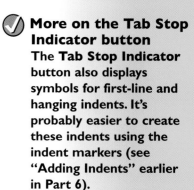

**(5)** Click at the desired location on the ruler to insert the tab.

**(6)** Press **Tab** to move to the first tab stop, and type your text. Then press **Tab** to get to next tab stop (if any) and type your text.

**(7)** Press **Enter** after typing the last block of text on the line, and type the remaining paragraphs that use the custom tabs.

**(8)** Remember that the **Show/Hide** button lets you see where you pressed the Tab key (refer to "Seeing Paragraph, Tab, and Space Marks" in Part 3).

✓ **More on the Tab Stop Indicator button**
The **Tab Stop Indicator** button also displays symbols for first-line and hanging indents. It's probably easier to create these indents using the indent markers (see "Adding Indents" earlier in Part 6).

End Task

# Task 9: Setting a Custom Center or Decimal Tab

## Setting a Custom Center or Decimal Tab

Setting custom center and decimal tabs is exactly the same as setting left and right tabs. Center tabs let you center text over the tab stop, and decimal tabs align text along the decimal point. (Decimal tabs are most useful for typing columns of numbers.) If you haven't already done so, look over the preceding task to get an overview of working with custom tabs before continuing with these steps.

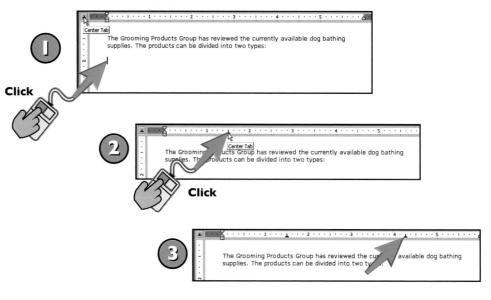

Start Here

Click

Click

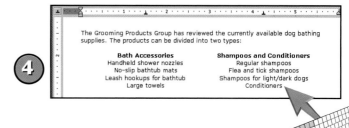

✓ **What is a bar tab?**
A bar tab creates a vertical line at the tab stop. You can use it to add vertical lines to divide columns of text on your page. In general, however, it's easier to create vertical lines with the Tables feature (see Part 9).

1. To insert a center tab, display the center-tab symbol on the **Tab Stop Indicator** button, and click in the paragraph where you want to use the tab.

2. Click at the desired location on the ruler to insert the tab.

3. Insert any additional tabs in the paragraph. In this example, a second center tab was added to the right.

4. Type your text using the custom tabs (see steps 6 and 7 in the preceding task).

Next Step

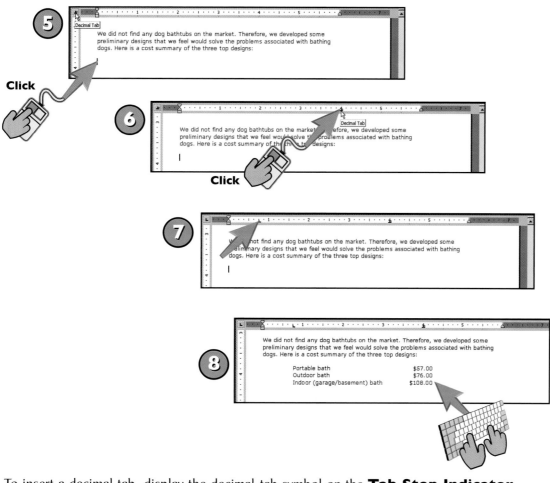

**Click**

**Click**

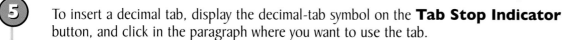

**5** To insert a decimal tab, display the decimal-tab symbol on the **Tab Stop Indicator** button, and click in the paragraph where you want to use the tab.

**6** Click at the desired location on the ruler to insert the tab.

**7** Insert any additional tabs in the paragraph. In this example, a left tab was added to the left of the decimal tab.

**8** Again, type your text using the custom tabs as described in steps 6 and 7 in the preceding task.

End Task

## Moving and Deleting a Custom Tab

When you work with custom tabs, you will frequently need to adjust their positions on the ruler. If you've already typed your text, it shifts as soon as you move the tab. Deleting a custom tab is even simpler: You just drag it off of the ruler.

✓ **Restoring default tab settings**
To restore the default tabs below a paragraph that contains custom tabs, click in the paragraph where you'd like the default tabs to begin, and delete the custom tabs as described in these steps. The default tabs will automatically reappear.

# Task 10: Moving and Deleting a Custom Tab

**Start Here**

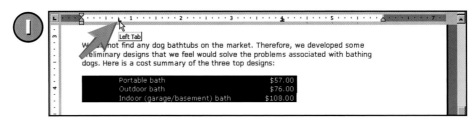

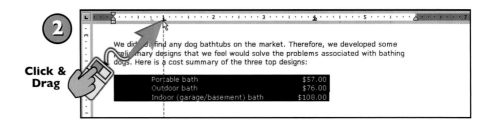

Click & Drag

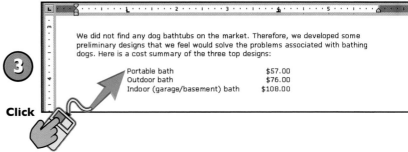

Click

1. To move a custom tab, select the paragraphs that contain the tab, and point to it on the ruler.

2. Drag the tab to the new position. A vertical dotted line shows you where the text will realign.

3. Release the mouse button and click to deselect the text. The text shifts to the repositioned tab.

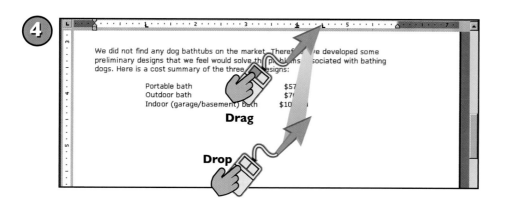

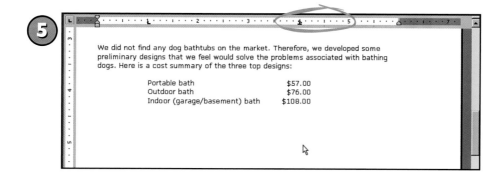

**4** To delete a tab, point to it on the ruler and drag it straight down toward your document. Release the mouse button and click to deselect the text.

**5** The tab is no longer on the ruler.

# Task 11: Adding a Border to a Paragraph

## Adding a Border

You don't have to know anything about graphics to set off paragraphs with attractive borders, and you can even add a decorative border around the whole page. In this task, you learn how to add a border. In the next task, you learn how to further enhance the appearance of a paragraph with shading, which adds a background color to the paragraph.

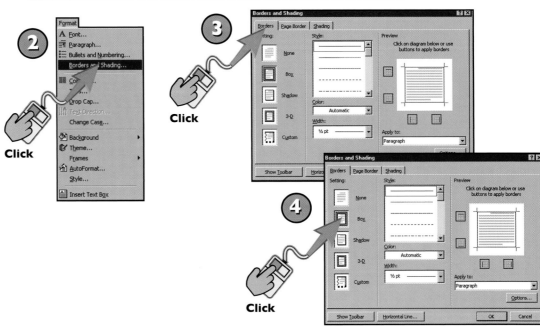

Click

Click

Click

Click

 **Indent the left and right borders**
If you don't want the right and left borders on a paragraph to extend all the way to the margins, set left and right indents (see "Adding Indents" earlier in Part 6).

(1) Select the paragraphs to which you want to add the border.

(2) Choose **Format, Borders and Shading** to display the Borders and Shading dialog box.

(3) Click the **Borders** tab if it isn't already in front.

(4) Click the type of border that most closely matches what you want under **Setting**.

 Next Step

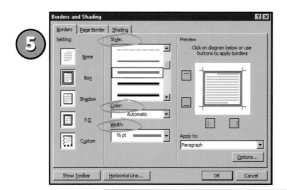

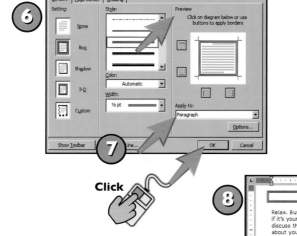

**Click**

---

**Removing borders
from a paragraph**
To remove borders from
a paragraph, select the
paragraph, choose
**Format, Borders and
Shading**, click the **Borders**
tab, click **None** under
**Setting**, and click **OK**.

**Adding a border
around the entire page**
To add a border around
your entire page, click the
**Page Border** tab in the
Borders and Shading dialog
box, and then select from
the same set of options as
those in the **Borders** tab.

**5**    Choose the options you like in the **Style**, **Color**, and **Width** lists.

**6**    The **Preview** area shows the options you've chosen.

**7**    Make sure that it says **Paragraph** in the **Apply to** list, and then click **OK**.

**8**    Word applies your borders to the selected paragraphs.

End
Task

# Task 12: Shading a Paragraph

## Shading a Paragraph

**If you really want to set off a paragraph or two from the rest of your text, adding shading might do the trick. For additional emphasis, you can also add borders as described in the preceding task.**

Start Here

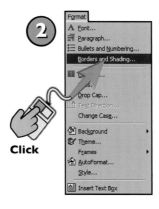

Tips for the First-Time Home Buyer

Relax. Buying home is stressful for anyone, and it is all the more anxiety-producing if it's your first time. Jot down all of your questions as you think of them, and then discuss them one-by-one with your real estate agent. Don't be afraid to be assertive about your concerns. If something about the house or the contract doesn't look right to you, it probably isn't.

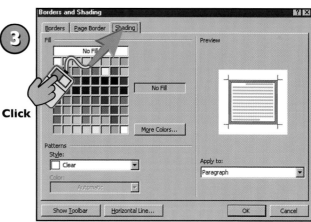

**Format**

A Font...
Paragraph...
Bullets and Numbering...
Borders and Shading...

Drop Cap...
Text Direction...
Change Case...

Background
Theme...
Frames
AutoFormat...
Style...

Insert Text Box

**Click**

**Borders and Shading**

Borders | Page Border | Shading

Fill
No Fill

No Fill

More Colors...

Patterns
Style:
Clear
Color:
Automatic

Preview

Apply to:
Paragraph

Show Toolbar | Horizontal Line... | OK | Cancel

**Click**

---

① Select the paragraphs to which you want to add shading.

② Choose **Format, Borders and Shading** to display the Borders and Shading dialog box.

③ Click the **Shading** tab.

Next Step

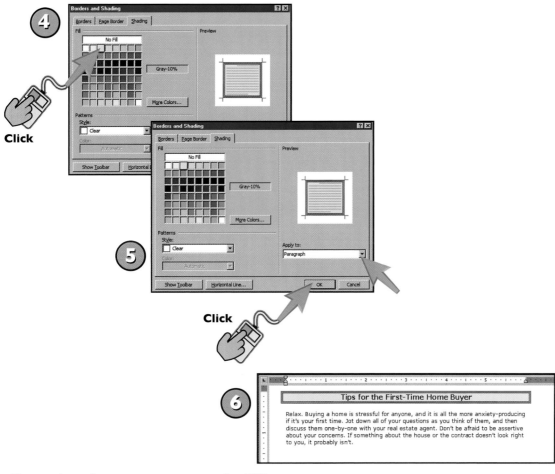

**Click**

**Click**

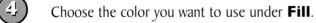

Tips for the First-Time Home Buyer

Relax. Buying a home is stressful for anyone, and it is all the more anxiety-producing if it's your first time. Jot down all of your questions as you think of them, and then discuss them one-by-one with your real estate agent. Don't be afraid to be assertive about your concerns. If something about the house or the contract doesn't look right to you, it probably isn't.

(4) Choose the color you want to use under **Fill**.

(5) Make sure that it says **Paragraph** in the **Apply to** list, and then click **OK**.

(6) The shading is applied to the selected paragraphs.

# Task 13: Copying Font and Paragraph Formatting

## Copying Formatting

If you have carefully applied several font or paragraph formats to a block of text and then decide that you'd like to use the same combination of formats somewhere else in the document, you don't have to apply the formatting from scratch. Instead, you can use Word's Format Painter feature to copy the formatting of the original block of text and then "paint" it across the other text. Follow steps 1 through 4 if you only want to copy font formatting, or steps 5 through 8 to copy paragraph and font formatting.

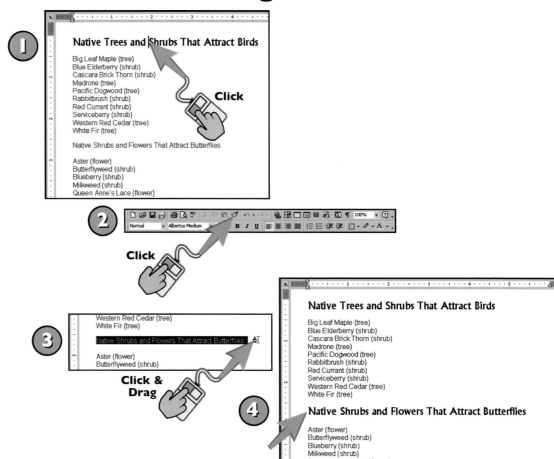

1. To copy just the font formatting, click anywhere in the text that has the formatting you want to copy.

2. Click the **Format Painter** button on the Formatting toolbar.

3. The mouse pointer becomes an I-beam with a paintbrush attached to it. Drag over the text where you want to apply the formatting.

4. Release the mouse button. Word applies the formatting to the selected text.

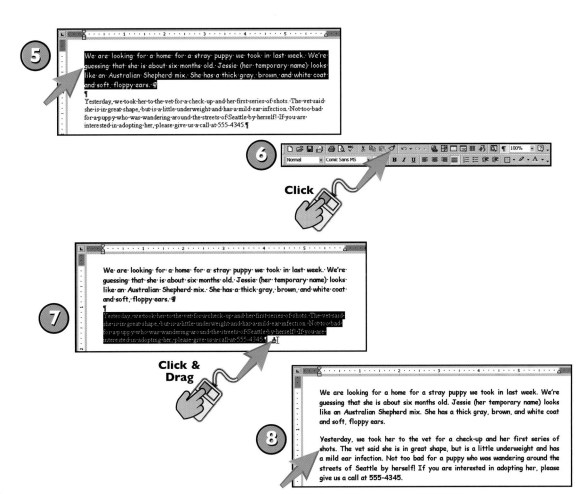

**Click**

**Click &
Drag**

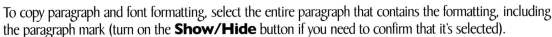

5    To copy paragraph and font formatting, select the entire paragraph that contains the formatting, including the paragraph mark (turn on the **Show/Hide** button if you need to confirm that it's selected).

6    Click the **Format Painter** button on the Formatting toolbar.

7    The mouse pointer becomes an I-beam with a paintbrush attached to it. Drag over the paragraph to which you want to apply the formatting.

8    Release the mouse button. Word applies the formatting to the selected paragraph.

**Copying formatting to more than one place**
If you want to apply the same formatting to several blocks of text, double-click the **Format Painter** toolbar button. The Format Painter will stay turned on while you drag over multiple blocks of text. When you're finished, click the button again to turn it off.

**End Task**

# Formatting Pages

In the preceding part, you learned how to format characters and paragraphs. In this part, you learn how to apply formatting that affects entire pages. You'll start with changing margins, and then go on to inserting page breaks, centering a page vertically, and numbering pages. Finally, you learn how to create headers and footers—in other words, text that appears at the top or bottom of every page in your document.

# Tasks

# Task 1: Changing Margins

## Changing Margin Settings

Word's default margins are 1 inch on the top and bottom of the page and 1.25 inches on the left and right. You may want to decrease the margins if you need to squeeze a bit more text onto the page, or increase them to give your document a more spacious feel. When you change the margins, Word applies the new setting to all of the pages in your document.

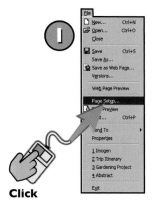

**Click**

**Click**

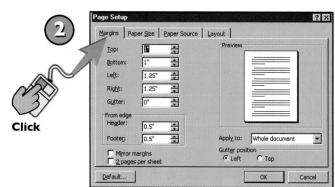

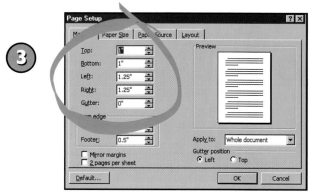

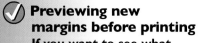 **Previewing new margins before printing**
If you want to see what your margins will look like before you print, use Print Layout view, Print Preview, or change the Zoom setting to Whole Page (see "Previewing a Document" and "Zooming a Document" in Part 5).

① Choose **File**, **Page Setup**. (It doesn't matter where your insertion point is.)

② In the Page Setup dialog box, click the **Margins** tab if it isn't already in front.

③ The **Top**, **Bottom**, **Left**, and **Right** text boxes let you change the width of all four margins.

Next Step

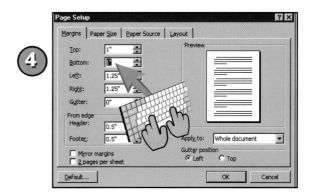

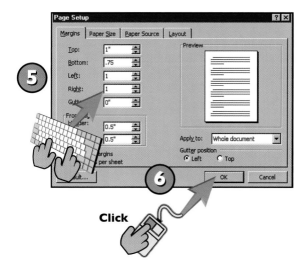

**Click**

④ Select the number in the text box for the margin you want to change. Type over the number with a new number in inches. (You don't have to type the " symbol.)

⑤ Repeat step 4 to change any other margins.

⑥ Click the **OK** button.

✓ **Changing paper orientation**
If you like, you can change the *orientation* of your document from the default *portrait* to *landscape*. Landscape orientation prints your document "sideways" across the paper, so that the long edge of the paper is the top of the page. To do this, click the **Paper Size** tab in the Page Setup dialog box, mark the **Landscape** option button, and click **OK**.

End Task

# Task 2: Inserting a Page Break

## Inserting a Page Break

When you fill a page with text, Word inserts a *soft page break* to end the page and wrap text to the next page. There are times, however, when you need to end a page before it's filled with text. To do this, you insert a *hard page break*. For example, you can use a hard page break to separate a title page from the text that follows or to start a new section of a report at the top of the next page.

✓ **Previewing page breaks**

You can see the results of inserting a hard page break most clearly by switching to Print Preview or by changing the zoom setting in Print Layout view to Whole Page. (See "Previewing a Document" and "Zooming a Document" in Part 5.)

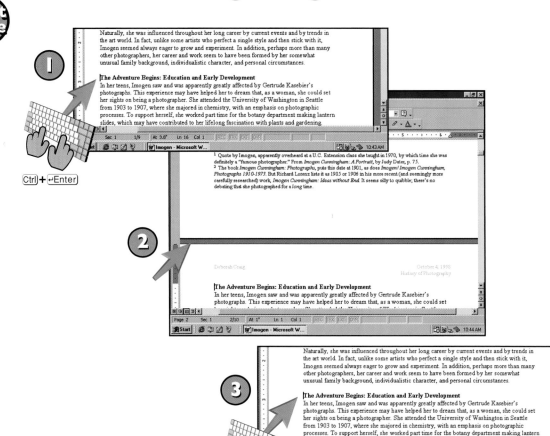

Start Here

Ctrl + ←Enter

←Backspace

① To insert a hard page break, click where you want to break the page and press **Ctrl+Enter**.

② Word inserts a hard page break at the insertion point and moves the text below the break onto the next page.

③ If you need to remove a hard page break, click at the beginning of the first line underneath the break, and press the **Backspace** key.

Next Step

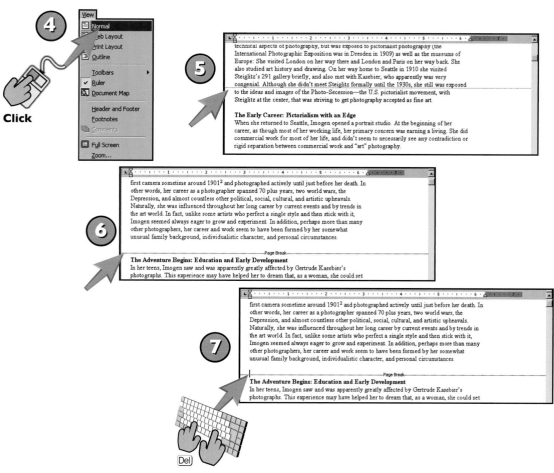

**Click**

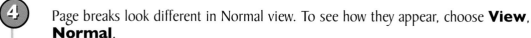

**4** Page breaks look different in Normal view. To see how they appear, choose **View**, **Normal**.

**5** In Normal view, a soft page break appears as a horizontal dotted line running across your document.

**6** A hard page break appears as a horizontal dotted line with the words *Page Break* in the middle of it.

**7** To remove a hard page break while in Normal view, click on the dotted line and press **Delete**.

End Task

# Task 3: Centering a Page Vertically

## Centering a Page Vertically

Many people try to center text vertically on the page by moving the insertion point to the top of the page and then pressing Enter several times to force the text down. More often than not, you end up pressing Enter too many (or too few) times, and then you have to add or delete blank lines to position the text where you want it. A more straightforward method is to let Word center the page vertically for you.

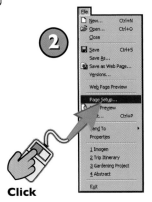

**Click**

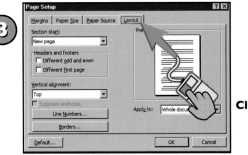

**Click**

1. Press the **Backspace** or **Delete** key to remove any blank lines from above and below the text you want to center vertically.

2. Choose **File**, **Page Setup** to display the Page Setup dialog box.

3. Click the **Layout** tab if it isn't already in front.

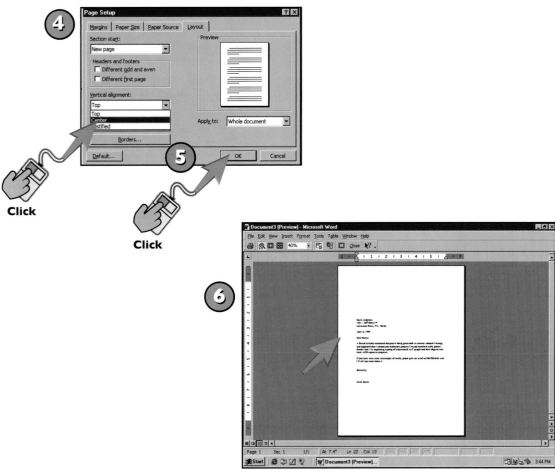

**Click**

**Click**

④ Click the **down arrow** to the right of the **Vertical alignment** list, and click **Center**.

⑤ Click the **OK** button.

⑥ If you like, preview the document in Print Preview before printing.

# Task 4: Numbering Pages

## Adding Page Numbers

Word offers two methods for adding page numbers to your document. First, you can use the **Insert, Page Numbers** command, as described in this task, to tell Word what type of page number you want and where it should appear. Word then adds the page number *field* to the header or footer for you. Second, you can enter the page number field by inserting it directly in the header or footer (see the next two tasks). This second method gives you more control over the appearance of your page numbers.

**Click**

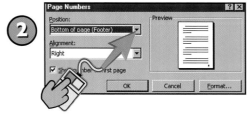

**Click**

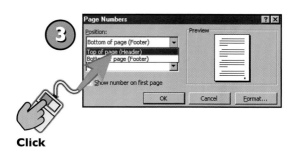

**Click**

✓ **Viewing page numbers**
Page numbers are visible in Print Layout view and Print Preview. They aren't, however, visible in Normal view.

① Choose **Insert**, **Page Numbers**.

② If you want the number at the bottom of the page, skip to step 4. To place the number at the top of the page, click the **down arrow** next to the **Position** list.

③ Choose **Top of page (Header)**.

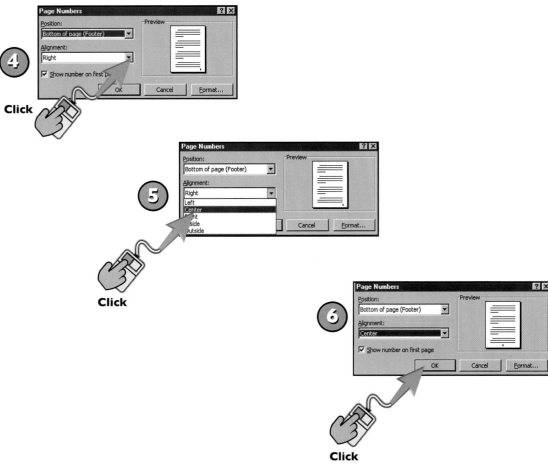

**Click**

**Click**

**Click**

4 Click the **down arrow** to the right of the **Alignment** list.

5 Choose the alignment you prefer for your page numbers.

6 Click the **OK** button.

# Task 5: Creating Headers and Footers

## Adding Headers and Footers to Your Document

A header appears at the top of every page, and a footer appears at the bottom of every page. You might want to use headers and footers to display the document title, your name, the name of your organization, and so on. In this task, you learn how to type standard text in your headers and footers. In the next task, you use the Header and Footer toolbar to insert fields that display information such as the page number and the current date.

✓ **Formatting the font in your headers and footers**

You can format the font and font size of your header and footer text just as you do standard text. Select the text and choose the formatting you want from the Font and Font Size drop-down lists in the Formatting toolbar. (See "Changing the Font and Font Size" in Part 6.)

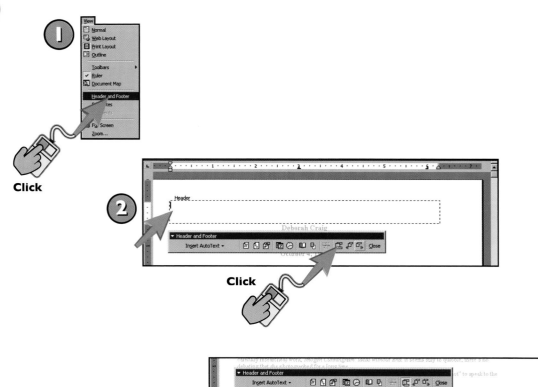

Click

Click

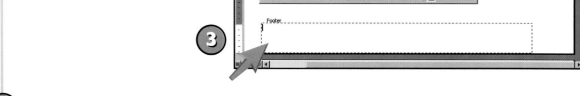

1. Choose **View, Header and Footer**. (It doesn't matter where your insertion point is when you issue the command.)

2. Word activates the header area and displays the Header and Footer toolbar. Click the **Switch Between Header and Footer** button.

3. Word activates the footer area. (Click the **Switch Between Header and Footer** button again when you want to switch back to the header area.)

Next Step

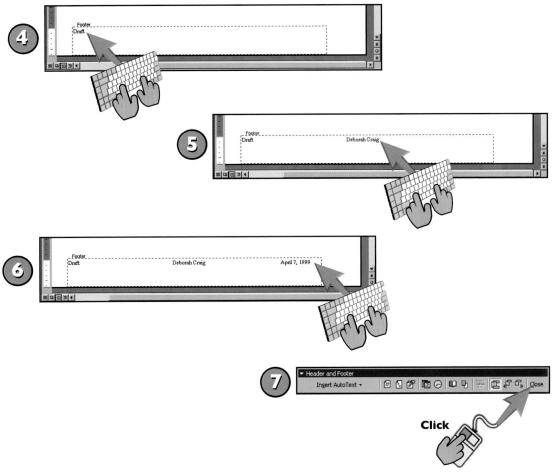

**Click**

4 Type any text that you want to appear at the left margin.

5 Press the **Tab** key to jump to a center tab in the center of the footer. Type any text that you want centered here.

6 Press the **Tab** key again to move to a right tab at the right edge of the footer. Type any text that you want flush right here.

7 Click the **Close** button in the Header and Footer toolbar to return to viewing your document text.

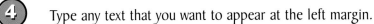

✅ **Viewing headers and footers**
You can see your headers and footers in Print Layout view (**View, Print Layout**) and Print Preview (**File, Print Preview**). They are not visible in Normal view.

**End Task**

# Task 6: Inserting Dates and Page Numbers in Headers and Footers

## Using the Header and Footer Toolbar

The Header and Footer toolbar makes it easy to insert commonly used blocks of text in a header or footer, as well as fields for the date, the page number, the time, and so on. Here, you take a quick tour of some of the options available on the toolbar. Feel free to experiment more on your own.

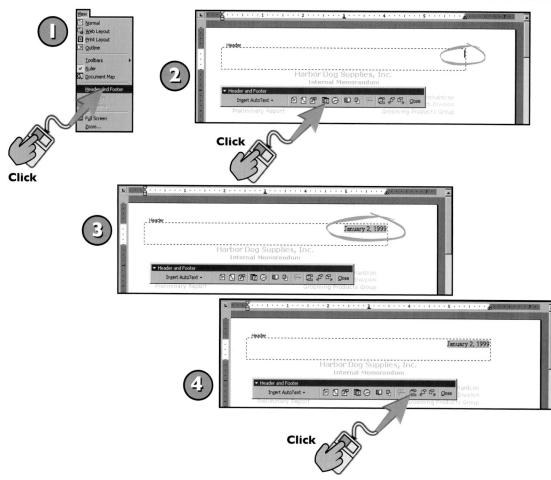

**Click**

**Click**

**Click**

✅ **Deleting fields**
To delete a field, select it by double-clicking it or dragging over it with the mouse and then press the Delete key.

1. Choose **View**, **Header and Footer**.

2. Press **Tab** twice to move to the right edge of the header area, and click the **Insert Date** button.

3. Word inserts the current date. (To insert the current time, click the **Insert Time** button to the right of the **Insert Date** button.)

4. Click the **Switch Between Header and Footer** button to move to the footer area.

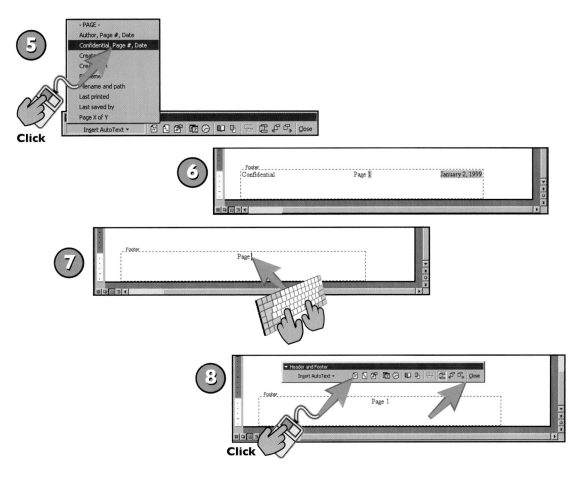

**Click**

**Click**

<table>
<tr><td>**5**</td><td>Click the **Insert AutoText** button, and then choose **Confidential, Page #, Date**.</td></tr>
<tr><td>**6**</td><td>Word inserts the AutoText entry in the footer. Select and delete this entry. Then try a few other AutoText entries, and delete the last one.</td></tr>
<tr><td>**7**</td><td>Press the **Tab** key, type **Page**, and then press the **Spacebar**.</td></tr>
<tr><td>**8**</td><td>Click the **Insert Page Number** button, and then click the **Close** button in the Header and Footer toolbar.</td></tr>
</table>

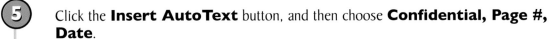

End Task

# Editing Timesavers

You don't *have* to use any of the features described in this part. But they sure can help. All of the skills you learn here will save you editing time and increase your efficiency. You learn how to ask Word to search a document for a particular word or phrase and replace it with something else, how to check your spelling and fix spelling errors automatically, how to insert the date automatically, and much more.

# Tasks

# Task 1: Searching for Text

## Searching for Text

If you frequently type long documents, you have probably had the experience of scrolling through each page trying to find all the places where you used a particular word or phrase. Word can help you with this process, searching for text much more quickly and accurately than we humans can.

**Start Here**

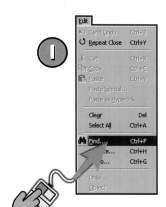

**Click**

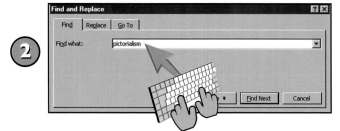

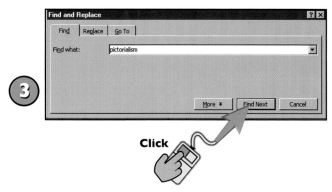

**Click**

✓ **Using more options in your search**
If you want to be more specific about what text you're looking for, click the **More** button at the bottom of the Find and Replace dialog box to display more options. To hide the options again, click the **Less** button.

① Choose **Edit**, **Find** to display the **Find** tab of the Find and Replace dialog box.

② Type the text that you want to find in the **Find what** text box.

③ Click the **Find Next** button.

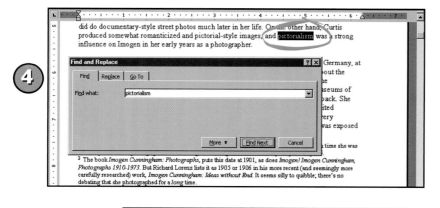

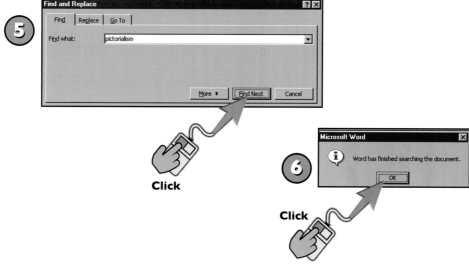

**Click**

**Click**

**4** Word highlights the first occurrence of the word.

**5** Continue to click the **Find Next** button to look for more matches.

**6** Click **OK** when Word informs you that it has finished searching the document, and then click the **Cancel** button in the Find and Replace dialog box.

# Task 2: Finding and Replacing Text

## Finding and Replacing Text

Sometimes you need not only to find text, you also have to replace it with something else. Word's Replace feature takes the tedium out of making the same change in several places. Whenever you find yourself about to change something by hand throughout your entire document, stop and see whether you could have Replace do the work for you.

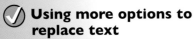

**Using more options to replace text**

If you want to be more specific about what text you're looking for, click the **More** button at the bottom of the Find and Replace dialog box to display more options. To hide the options again, click the **Less** button.

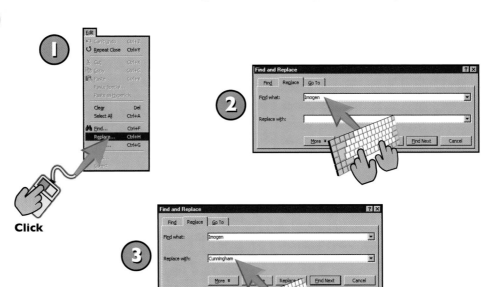

**Click**

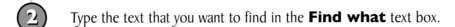

**Click**

1. Choose **Edit**, **Replace** to display the **Replace** tab of the Find and Replace dialog box.

2. Type the text that you want to find in the **Find what** text box.

3. In the **Replace with** text box, type the text that you want to replace the **Find what** text.

4. Click the **Find Next** button.

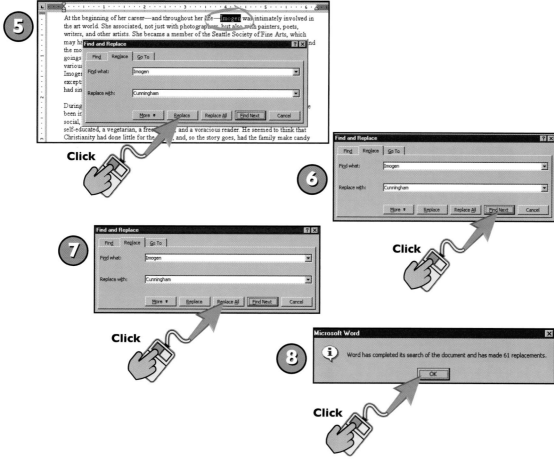

**Click**

**Click**

**Click**

**Click**

**5** Word highlights the first occurrence of the word. To replace it, click the **Replace** button.

**6** To skip this instance without making the change, click the **Find Next** button.

**7** Continue this process. If you don't need to confirm every replacement, click the **Replace All** button.

**8** Click **OK** when Word informs you that it has finished searching the document, and then click the **Close** button in the Find and Replace dialog box.

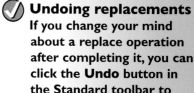 **Undoing replacements**
If you change your mind about a replace operation after completing it, you can click the **Undo** button in the Standard toolbar to undo the replacements one by one if you used the Replace button, or all at once if you used the Replace All button.

 **End Task**

# Using Automatic Spell Checking

Word's automatic spell checking monitors the characters you type and marks words not found in its dictionary with red wavy lines. (By default, Word also checks your grammar and highlights possible problems with green wavy lines, but you can turn off the grammar checking and check only the spelling.) Automatic spell checking enables you to fix misspellings as you're typing. To correct spelling after you've typed the entire document, see the next task.

# Task 3: Using Automatic Spell Checking

**Start Here**

**1**
Relax. Buying a home is stressfull for anyone, and it is all the more anxiety-producing if it's your first time. Jot down all of your questions as you think of them, and then discuss them one-by-one with your real estate agent. Don't be afraid to be assertive about your concerns. If something about the house or the contract doesn't look right to you, it probably isn't.

**Right Click**

**2**
Relax. Buying a home is stressfull for anyone, and it is all the more anxiety-producing if it's your first time. Jot down all of them, and then discuss them one-by-one with your real ... be afraid to be assertive about your concerns. If something about t... ract doesn't look right to you, it probably isn't.

stressful
stressfully

Ignore All
Add

AutoCorrect ▶
Language ▶
Spelling...

**Click**

**3**
Relax. Buying a home is stressful for anyone, and it is all the more anxiety-producing if it's your first time. Jot down all of your questions as you think of them, and then discuss them one-by-one with your real estate agent. Don't be afraid to be assertive about your concerns. If something about the house or the contract doesn't look right to you, it probably isn't.

**4**
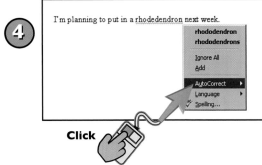

**Click**

---

**1** To correct the spelling of a word marked with a red wavy line, right-click the word.

**2** A context menu appears with a list of possible spellings. If you see the one you want, click it.

**3** Word makes the correction for you.

**4** If the mistake is one you frequently make, point to **AutoCorrect**.

**Next Step**

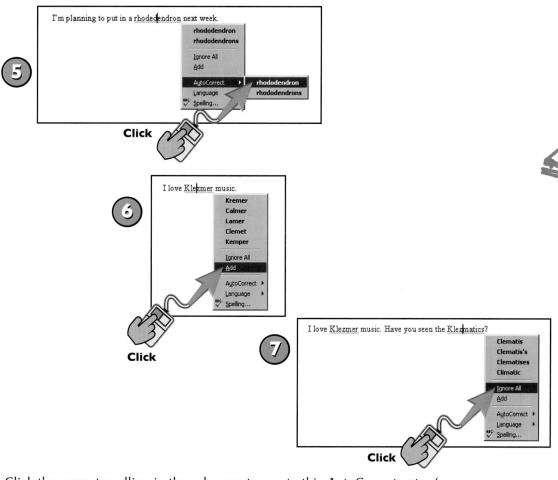

I'm planning to put in a rhododendron next week.

rhododendron
rhododendrons

Ignore All
Add

AutoCorrect ▶    rhododendron
Language          rhododendrons
Spelling...

**Click**

**5**

I love Klezmer music.

Kremer
Calmer
Lamer
Clemet
Kemper

Ignore All
Add

AutoCorrect ▶
Language   ▶
Spelling...

**6**

**Click**

I love Klezmer music. Have you seen the Klezmatics?

Clematis
Clematis's
Clematises
Climatic

Ignore All
Add

AutoCorrect ▶
Language   ▶
Spelling...

**7**

**Click**

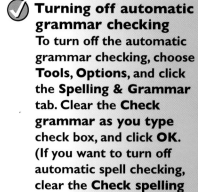

**5** Click the correct spelling in the submenu to create this AutoCorrect entry (see "Correcting Text Automatically" later in Part 8).

**6** If a word is spelled correctly and you use it frequently, click **Add** to add it to the dictionary so that Word won't catch it in the future.

**7** If a word is spelled correctly but you don't use it that often, choose **Ignore All** to prevent Word from marking it as a misspelling in this document only.

✓ **Turning off automatic grammar checking**
To turn off the automatic grammar checking, choose **Tools, Options,** and click the **Spelling & Grammar** tab. Clear the **Check grammar as you type** check box, and click **OK.** (If you want to turn off automatic spell checking, clear the **Check spelling as you type** check box.)

End Task

## Checking Your Spelling

The spell checker enables you to check the spelling (and grammar) of an entire document all at once. You won't really need to use it if you use automatic spell checking to fix your spelling "on the fly" (see the preceding task). However, if you've disabled automatic spell checking, or if you're working on a rather large document, the spell checker will come in handy.

**Turning off grammar checking**

If you don't want Word to look for grammatical problems during the spell check, clear the **Check grammar** check box in the lower-left corner of the Spelling and Grammar dialog box.

# Task 4: Checking Your Spelling with the Spell Checker

Start
Here

Click

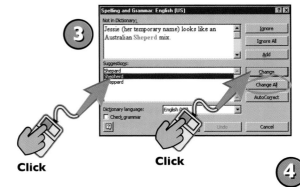

Click

Click

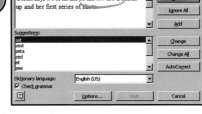

①  Click the **Spelling and Grammar** button on the Standard toolbar to start checking your document.

②  When Word finds a spelling error, it highlights it in red.

③  If you see the correct spelling, click it and click the **Change** button (or **Change All** to change it throughout the document).

④  Sometimes Word doesn't offer the correct spelling for a misspelled word.

Next
Step

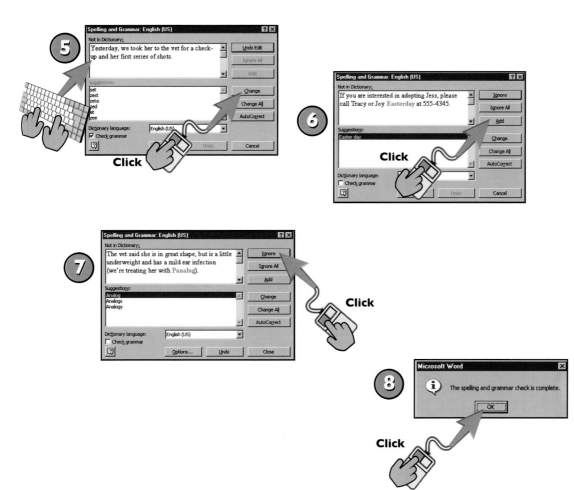

**5** If this happens, select the word, type over it with the correct spelling, and click the **Change** button.

**6** If the word is spelled correctly and you plan to use it often, click the **Add** button to add it to the dictionary.

**7** To leave the word as it appears, click **Ignore** to ignore it once or **Ignore All** to ignore it throughout the document.

**8** When Word tells you that it has finished the spell check, click **OK**.

# Task 5: Using the Thesaurus

## Looking for Other Word Choices

If you find yourself overusing a particular word and want to find a good synonym for it, or if you want to get some ideas for livening up your text, Word's thesaurus can help you out.

Start Here

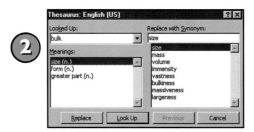

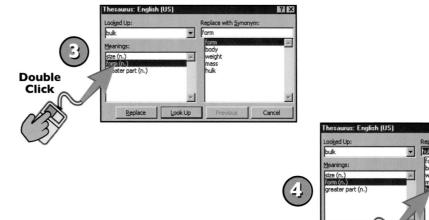

**Double Click**

**Double Click**

✓ **Looking up other words**

If you want to look up synonyms for a word that isn't in the Replace with Synonym list, select the current entry in the **Replace with Synonym** text box, type over it with the word whose synonyms you want to look up, and click the **Look Up** button.

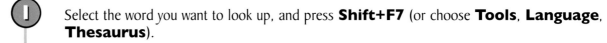

**1** Select the word you want to look up, and press **Shift+F7** (or choose **Tools**, **Language**, **Thesaurus**).

**2** Word displays the Thesaurus dialog box with the word you selected in the Looked Up list box.

**3** If the selected meaning in the Meanings list is not the one you need, double-click a different one.

**4** If you want to see the synonyms of a word in the synonyms list, double-click it.

Next Step

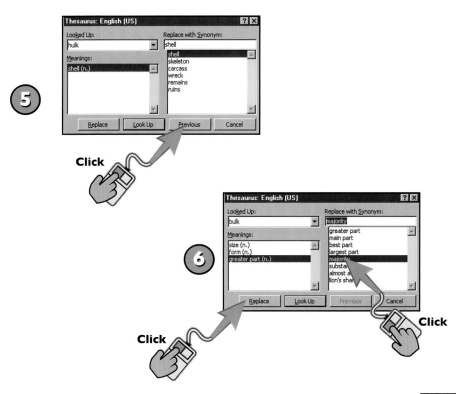

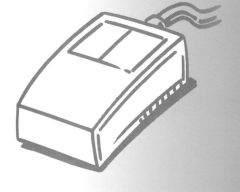

gardener her entire life, it was people rath
attention for the majority of her career. Pl
1920s and 1930s, and in some cases the in
inspired, works produced for the likes of
botanical subject and then moved on. Her
abstract—perhaps more in the Photo-Sec

**Click**

**Click**

**Click**

Word places the new word in the **Looked Up** list box and displays the synonyms for that word. If you want to go back to a previous definition, click the **Previous** button.

When you see the word that you want to use, click it and click the **Replace** button.

Word replaces the selected word with the one you chose.

**Installing the Thesaurus**
By default, the thesaurus is not installed until you use it for the first time. If you see a message box asking whether you'd like to install it, insert your **Office 2000 CD-ROM** and click the **Yes** button.

End Task

## Using Special Characters

Many everyday documents, such as letters and memos, require special characters here and there. For example, you might need to use the trademark symbol (™), a long dash (—), or the ellipses (...). As you'll see in steps 1 through 3, Word inserts many of these symbols for you automatically as you type. If it doesn't insert the one you need, you can likely find it in the Symbol dialog box.

 **Changing the size of symbols**

You can enlarge symbols that you've inserted in your document just like regular text. Drag over the symbol to select it, and then choose a larger point size from the **Font Size** drop-down list in the Formatting toolbar. (See "Changing the Font and Font Size" in Part 6.)

# Task 6: Inserting a Special Character

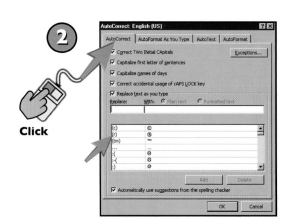

**Click**

**Click**

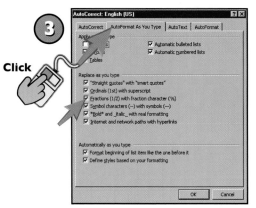

**Click**

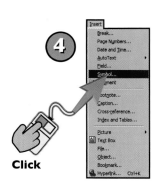

**Click**

 Choose **Tools, AutoCorrect** to display the AutoCorrect dialog box.

 Click the **AutoCorrect** tab. When you type the characters on the left, Word replaces them with the symbols on the right. (See "Correcting Text Automatically" later in Part 8.)

 Click the **AutoFormat As You Type** tab. The **Replace as you type** options insert many symbols for you as well. Click the **Cancel** button.

 To insert a less commonly used symbol, click where you want the symbol to go, and choose **Insert, Symbol**.

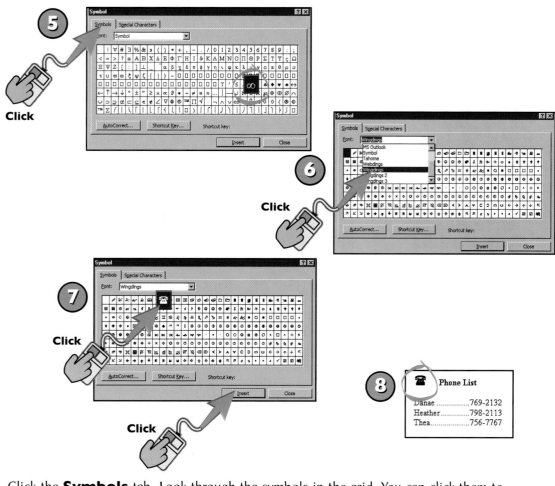

**Click**

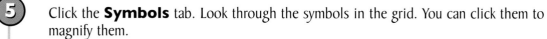

**Click**

**Click**

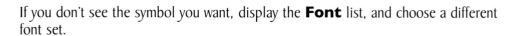

**Click**

 **Phone List**

Danae ...............769-2132
Heather.............798-2113
Thea.................756-7767

**5** Click the **Symbols** tab. Look through the symbols in the grid. You can click them to magnify them.

**6** If you don't see the symbol you want, display the **Font** list, and choose a different font set.

**7** To insert a symbol, click it, click the **Insert** button, and then click the **Close** button.

**8** Word inserts the symbol in your document.

**End Task**

# Task 7: Inserting the Date

## Adding a Date to Your Document

Your computer has a clock that keeps track of the date and the time. Instead of typing the current date, you can have Word take this information from the computer and insert it for you. You can even insert the date as a *field*, which enables Word to update it to the current date for you when you open the document in the future. Inserting a date as a field is useful in documents you open frequently because the date is always current. The drawback to doing this is that you don't have a date within the document verifying when it was first created and saved.

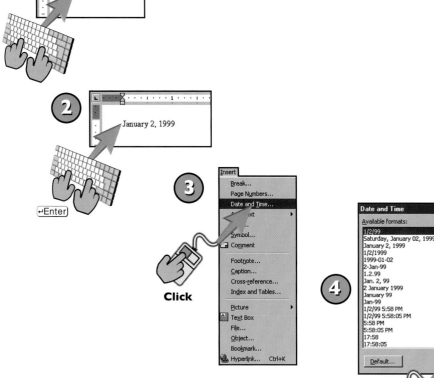

Click

Click

⊘ **Deleting the date field**
To delete a date that you've inserted as a field, select it first and then press **Delete** or **Backspace**.

Begin typing today's date. After you type a portion of the date, a yellow bubble containing the completed date appears.

Press **Enter** to let Word fill in the rest of the date for you.

If you want to insert the date as a field, choose **Insert**, **Date and Time**.

Mark the **Update automatically** check box.

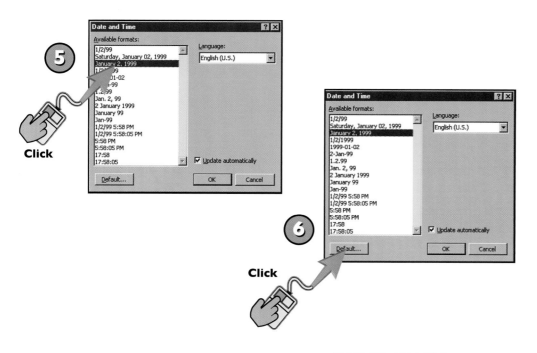

**Click**

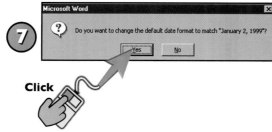

**Click**

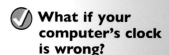

**Click**

**Click**

⑤ Click the date format that you want to use.

⑥ If you want to use this format all of the time, click the **Default** button.

⑦ Click **Yes** in the message box that appears, and click **OK** in the Date and Time dialog box. Word inserts the date in your document.

✓ **What if your computer's clock is wrong?**
If Word inserts the wrong date in your document, you have to correct your computer's clock. Double-click the time at the right end of the taskbar to display the **Date/Time Properties** dialog box. Specify the correct date in the **Date & Time** tab, and click **OK**.

End Task

# Task 8: Correcting Text Automatically

## Using AutoCorrect

**Word's AutoCorrect
feature fixes spelling errors
for you automatically. By
default, AutoCorrect makes
corrections based on
suggestions from the spell
checker. It also has its own
list of many commonly
misspelled words, and you
can add your own most
common typos to the list.
In addition, you can use
AutoCorrect to auto-
matically enter special
symbols, long names, or
phrases that you have to
type frequently.**

✓ **Using AutoCorrect to
insert repetitive text**

If you want to use
AutoCorrect to insert a
long name or phrase, type
an abbreviation for the
phrase in the **Replace** box
(see step 3), and type the
full spelling in the **With**
box (see step 4). For
example, you could type
`napf` in the **Replace** box
and `National Association
of Poodle Fanciers` in the
**With** box.

Start Here

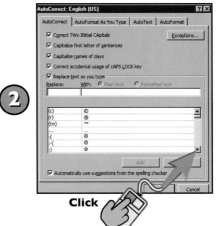

**Click**

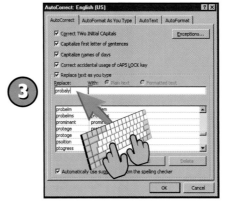

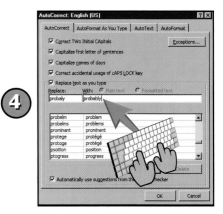

**Click**

① Choose **Tools, AutoCorrect**.

② Scroll down the list at the bottom of the dialog box to see what AutoCorrect knows how to fix. Word replaces the items in the left column with the items in the right column.

③ Click in the **Replace** text box and type **probaly**.

④ Click in the **With** text box and type the correct spelling, **probably**.

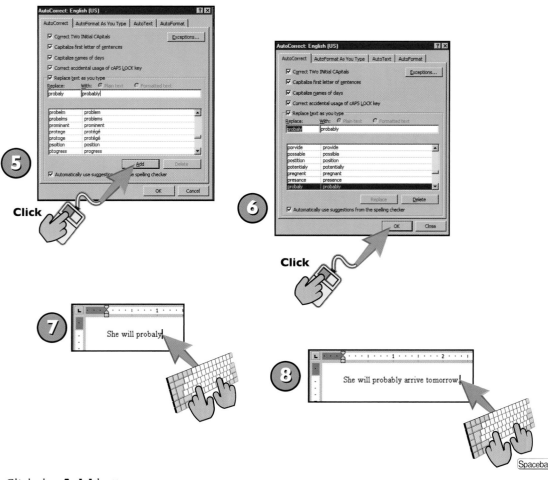

✔ **Removing AutoCorrect entries**
If you add an **AutoCorrect** entry and later decide to delete it, choose **Tools, AutoCorrect**, click the entry in the list in the **AutoCorrect** tab, click the **Delete** button, and click **OK**.

⚠ **Warning**
If you enter an abbreviation for a long name or phrase in the Replace box, choose one that you don't ever want to leave "as is" in your document, because Word will change it to the full "correct" spelling every time you type it.

**5**    Click the **Add** button.

**6**    The entry is added to the list. Click **OK**.

**7**    Type **She will probaly**.

**8**    Press the **Spacebar**. Word automatically replaces *probaly* with *probably*. Then finish the sentence as shown here.

# Task 9: Inserting Standard Blocks of Text

## Using AutoText

AutoText is an extremely handy feature that lets Word "memorize" large blocks of text. Once you've created an AutoText entry, you can insert it in your text by simply beginning to type the name of the entry. As soon as you've typed the first few characters, Word's AutoComplete feature takes over and inserts the entire block of text for you.

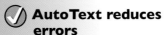 **AutoText reduces errors**

One of the advantages of using AutoText is that you only have to proofread the block of text once, before you create the AutoText entry. From then on, each time you insert the entry in a document, you can rest assured that it is error-free.

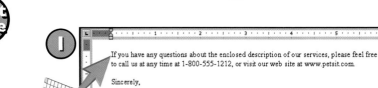

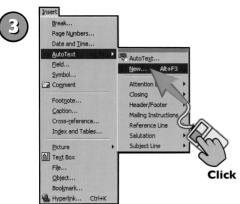

Click

Type the text that you want Word to "memorize."

Select the text.

Choose **Insert**, **AutoText**, **New**, or press **Alt+F3**.

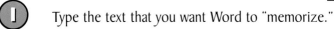

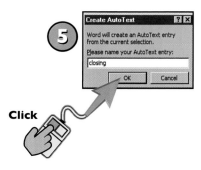

**Click**

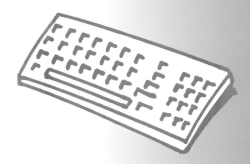

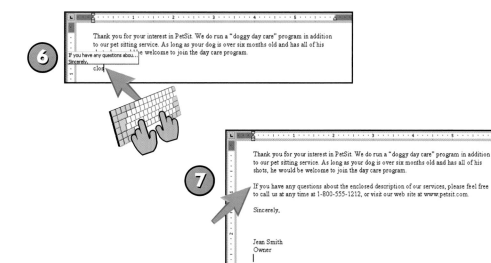

**4** Type a name for the entry in the Create AutoText dialog box. (Choose a name that is at least four characters long.)

**5** Click **OK**, and then click where you want to insert the text.

**6** Type the first few letters of the name. As soon as you see the yellow bubble, press **Enter**.

**7** Word inserts the AutoText entry in your document.

# Columns and Tables

In this part, you learn two different ways of arranging columns of text on the page. Word's columns feature lets you create "newspaper-style" columns, in which the text wraps from one column to the next. You might use columns for your office newsletter or a brochure. The tables feature, in contrast, is great for creating columns of text that do not wrap. Tables are useful for creating everything from simple charts to résumés and invoices.

# Tasks

# Task 1: Creating Columns

## Creating Columns in Your Document

If you would like to produce newsletters, bulletins, journal articles, and so on, you'll appreciate Word's ability to format text in multiple columns. When you use this feature, the text snakes from column to column. If you want to create columns of text that *do not* wrap from one column to the next, use either custom tabs (see Part 6) or a table (see the last four tasks in this part). If you don't want columns in part of your document, follow steps 1 through 5 to insert a *section break*. Otherwise, begin with step 6.

✓ **Changing the number of columns**
If you decide to change the number of columns in your document, simply repeat steps 6 through 8. If you want no columns, click the leftmost column in the grid in step 7.

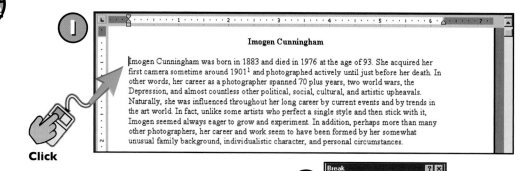

Click

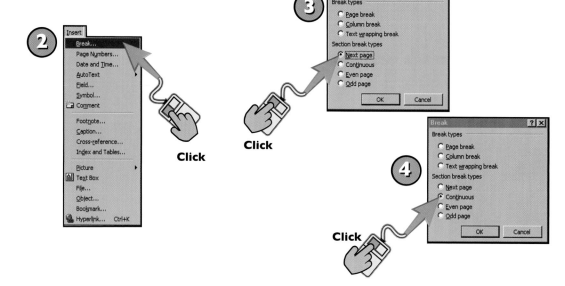

Click

Click

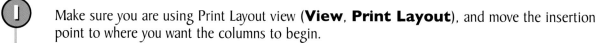

Click

① Make sure you are using Print Layout view (**View**, **Print Layout**), and move the insertion point to where you want the columns to begin.

② Choose **Insert**, **Break** to display the Break dialog box.

③ To make the columns begin at the top of a new page, choose **Next page**.

④ To keep the columns on the same page as the text above them, choose **Continuous**.

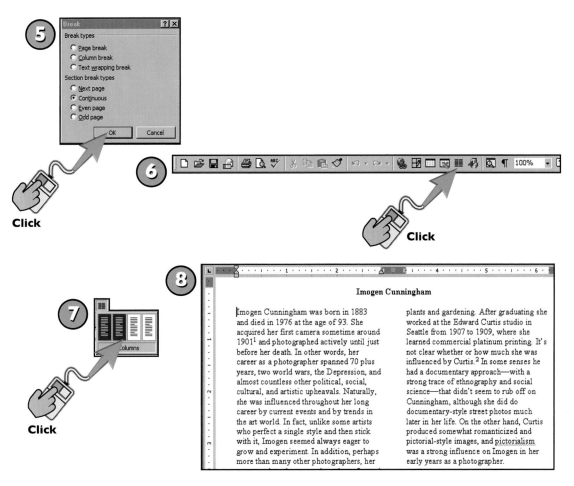

**Click**

**Click**

**Click**

The document shown reads:

**Imogen Cunningham**

Imogen Cunningham was born in 1883 and died in 1976 at the age of 93. She acquired her first camera sometime around 1901[1] and photographed actively until just before her death. In other words, her career as a photographer spanned 70 plus years, two world wars, the Depression, and almost countless other political, social, cultural, and artistic upheavals. Naturally, she was influenced throughout her long career by current events and by trends in the art world. In fact, unlike some artists who perfect a single style and then stick with it, Imogen seemed always eager to grow and experiment. In addition, perhaps more than many other photographers, her

plants and gardening. After graduating she worked at the Edward Curtis studio in Seattle from 1907 to 1909, where she learned commercial platinum printing. It's not clear whether or how much she was influenced by Curtis.[2] In some senses he had a documentary approach—with a strong trace of ethnography and social science—that didn't seem to rub off on Cunningham, although she did do documentary-style street photos much later in her life. On the other hand, Curtis produced somewhat romanticized and pictorial-style images, and pictorialism was a strong influence on Imogen in her early years as a photographer.

⑤ Click **OK**, and then make sure that your insertion point is in the section where you want the columns.

⑥ Click the **Columns** button on the Formatting toolbar.

⑦ Click the number of columns that you want in the grid.

⑧ Word creates the number of columns that you specified.

# Task 2: Formatting Columns

## Formatting Columns

In addition to the standard formatting options described in Parts 6 and 7 of this book, Word gives you a few other choices for formatting text in multiple columns. You can adjust the column widths, add vertical lines between columns, and so on. Try some of the options described here and see what works well in your documents.

**Start Here**

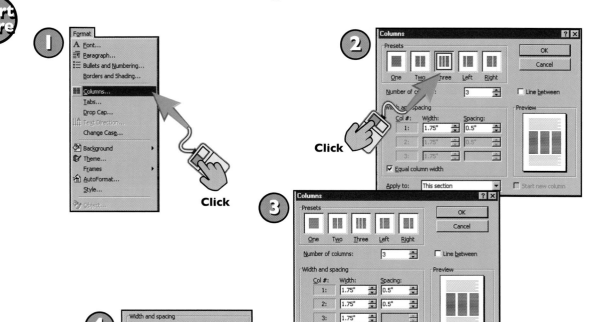

Click

Click

Click

Click

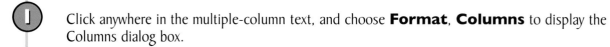

✓ **Justifying text in columns**

Columns often look better if the text is justified so that it also has a straight right edge. Select the column text, and click the **Justify** button in the Formatting toolbar. If you justify your text, it will probably look best if you hyphenate it as well.

① Click anywhere in the multiple-column text, and choose **Format**, **Columns** to display the Columns dialog box.

② If you like, click a preset format under **Presets** at the top of the dialog box.

③ If you have specific requirements for column widths, first clear the **Equal column width** check box.

④ Then enter the desired settings for each column under **Width and spacing**.

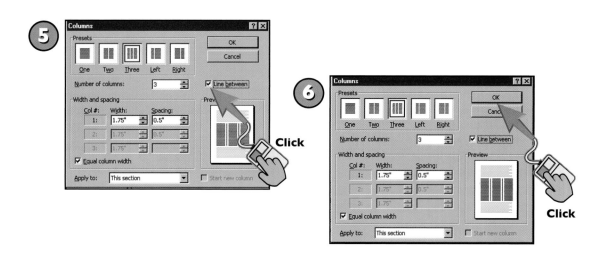

**Click**

**Click**

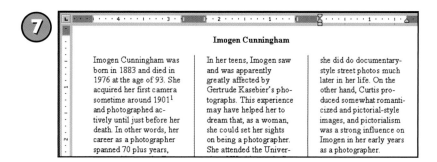

**Imogen Cunningham**

Imogen Cunningham was born in 1883 and died in 1976 at the age of 93. She acquired her first camera sometime around 1901[1] and photographed actively until just before her death. In other words, her career as a photographer spanned 70 plus years,

In her teens, Imogen saw and was apparently greatly affected by Gertrude Kasebier's photographs. This experience may have helped her to dream that, as a woman, she could set her sights on being a photographer. She attended the Univer-

she did do documentary-style street photos much later in her life. On the other hand, Curtis produced somewhat romanticized and pictorial-style images, and pictorialism was a strong influence on Imogen in her early years as a photographer.

**(5)** To add vertical lines between your columns, mark the **Line between** check box.

**(6)** When you have made all of your selections, click **OK**.

**(7)** Word applies the settings you chose to your text.

✅ **Hyphenating words**
If you are using narrow columns, you might want to hyphenate your text so that it fills the columns more evenly. Hyphenation also reduces the gaps between words in justified text. Choose **Tools, Language, Hyphenation,** mark the **Automatically hyphenate document** check box, and click **OK**.

✅ **Balancing the length of columns**
To balance the length of your columns on the last page of a document, press **Ctrl+End** to move to the end of the document, and choose **Insert, Break.** Mark the **Continuous** option button, and click **OK**.

# Task 3: Creating a Table

## Creating a Table

Word's table feature gives you a wonderfully flexible way of aligning text in a grid of rows and columns. You enter text into the individual boxes in the grid, which are referred to as *cells*. In this task, you learn to create a table using the **Insert Table** button on the Standard toolbar. In addition, you find out how to delete a table, in case you insert one that's not quite right and want to start over.

Start Here

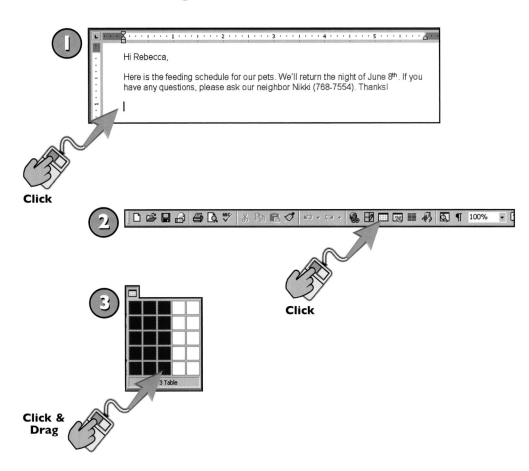

① Hi Rebecca,

Here is the feeding schedule for our pets. We'll return the night of June 8th. If you have any questions, please ask our neighbor Nikki (768-7554). Thanks!

**Click**

② **Click**

③ 3 Table

**Click & Drag**

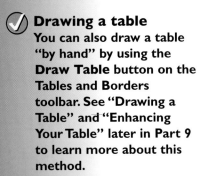

✓ **Drawing a table**

You can also draw a table "by hand" by using the **Draw Table** button on the Tables and Borders toolbar. See "Drawing a Table" and "Enhancing Your Table" later in Part 9 to learn more about this method.

① Move the insertion point to the place where you want to insert the table.

② Click the **Insert Table** button on the Standard toolbar.

③ The squares in the grid represent cells. Drag through the approximate number of rows and columns that you want, and then release the mouse button.

Next Step

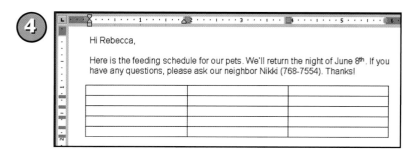

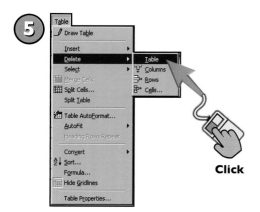

**Click**

(4) A table with the number of rows and columns you specified appears in the document.

(5) If you inserted a table accidentally and want to start over, verify that the insertion point is in the table, and choose **Table**, **Delete**, **Table**.

(6) The table is deleted from your document.

## Entering Text in a Table

Typing text in a table is much like typing in a regular document, but navigating within a table is somewhat different. In this task, you first learn how to move the insertion point from cell to cell within a table, and then you get a few pointers about entering text.

**Adding text above a table**

If you start a table at the very top of a document and then decide to insert text above the table, click at the far left edge of the upper-left cell in the table and press **Enter**. Word inserts a blank line above the table, and you can now click in the blank line and type your text.

# Task 4: Entering Text in a Table

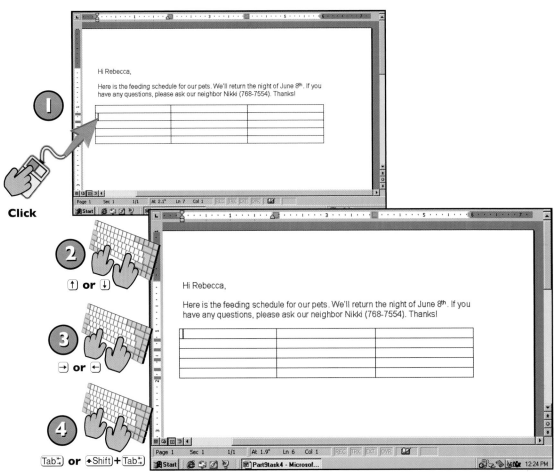

**Click**

↑ or ↓

→ or ←

Tab⇄ or Shift+Tab⇄

1. To move to a particular cell with the mouse, just click in the cell.

2. To move to the row above or below, press the **up-** or **down-arrow** key.

3. To move to the cell to the right or left, press the **right-** or **left-arrow** keys. (If there is text in a cell, these arrow keys move the insertion point through the text.)

4. You can also press the **Tab** key to move into the cell to the right or **Shift+Tab** to move to the left. (If the destination cell contains text, it will get selected.)

Next Step

|  | Morning | Evening |
|---|---|---|
| Joss (black male Standard Poodle) | 1 ½ cups of adult Nutramax | 1 ½ cups of adult Nutramax |
| Sneaker (white male Standard Poodle) | 2 cups of puppy Nutramax | 2 cups of puppy Nutramax |
| Sapphire (cat) | Max Cat senior cat kibble | Max Cat senior cat kibble and a little yogurt |
| Fish | A pinch of Total Tropical | A pinch of Total Tropical and a disc for the bottom-feeder |

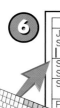

|  | Morning | Evening |
|---|---|---|
| Joss (black male Standard Poodle) | 1 ½ cups of adult Nutramax | 1 ½ cups of adult Nutramax |
| Sneaker (white male Standard Poodle) | 2 cups of puppy Nutramax | 2 cups of puppy Nutramax |
| Sapphire (cat) | Max Cat senior cat kibble | Max Cat senior cat kibble and a little yogurt |
| Fish | A pinch of Total Tropical | A pinch of Total Tropical and a disc for the bottom-feeder |

⏎Enter

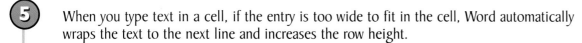

|  | Morning | Evening |
|---|---|---|
| Joss (black male Standard Poodle) | 1 ½ cups of adult Nutramax | 1 ½ cups of adult Nutramax |
| Sneaker (white male Standard Poodle) | 2 cups of puppy Nutramax | 2 cups of puppy Nutramax |
| Sapphire (cat) | nior cat | Max Cat senior cat kibble and a little yogurt |
| Fish | otal Tropical | A pinch of Total Tropical and a disc for the bottom-feeder |

←Backspace

(5) When you type text in a cell, if the entry is too wide to fit in the cell, Word automatically wraps the text to the next line and increases the row height.

(6) Press **Enter** in a cell to end the paragraph and add a blank line to that row.

(7) If you accidentally press Enter in a cell and want to remove the blank line, just press the **Backspace** key.

✓ **Inserting a tab within a cell**
**If you want to insert a tab within a cell, press Ctrl+Tab instead of Tab. (Pressing the Tab key by itself just selects the contents of the cell to the right.)**

End Task

## Changing the Table Structure

As you enter text in a table, you will probably need to change its structure. This task describes the most common adjustments you'll need to make. As you experiment with these techniques, keep in mind that Word does not prevent you from making a table too wide to fit on the page. If you're adding columns and increasing column widths, check Print Preview periodically to make sure that table isn't running off the page.

### ✅ Why are all of the Table menu commands dim?

Most of the commands in the Table menu are only active when the insertion point is in a table. If you notice that the commands are dim, it's a sign you accidentally clicked outside the table. Simply click inside the table and then display the Table menu again.

# Task 5: Adding, Deleting, and Resizing Rows and Columns

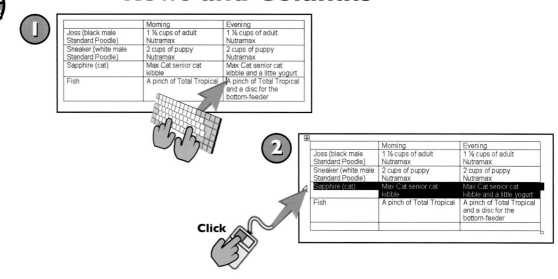

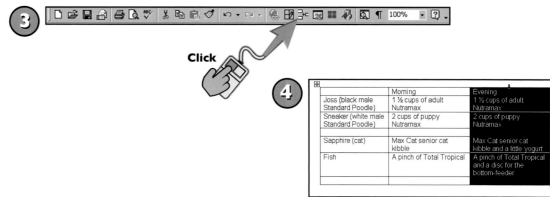

**1** To add a row at the end of the table, click anywhere in the lower-right cell in the table and press the Tab key.

**2** To add a row in the middle of the table, select the row below the location of the new one by clicking to its left, just outside of the table.

**3** Then click the **Insert Rows** button on the Standard toolbar. (The Insert Table button turns into Insert Rows when a row is selected.)

**4** To insert a column, select the column to the right of where the new one will go by clicking at the top of the column when the mouse pointer changes to a black arrow.

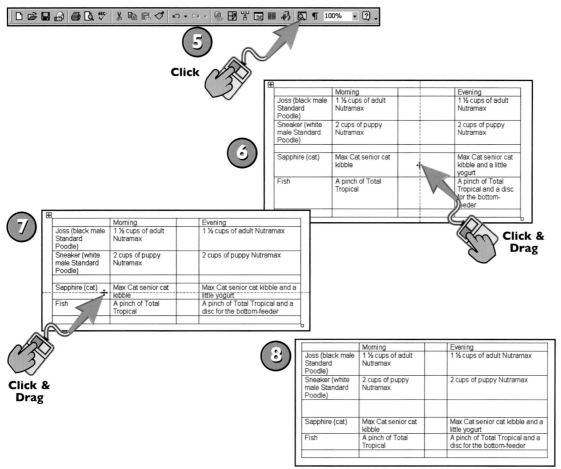

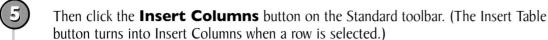

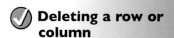

**5** Then click the **Insert Columns** button on the Standard toolbar. (The Insert Table button turns into Insert Columns when a row is selected.)

**6** To adjust a column's width, point to its right border and drag it to the desired location.

**7** To resize a row, point to its bottom border and drag it to the desired location.

**8** Make other changes to the table structure as needed.

**Deleting a row or column**

To delete a row or column, select it first (see steps 2 and 4), and then choose **Table, Delete, Rows** or **Table, Delete, Columns**.

# Task 6: Formatting a Table

## Formatting a Table

Formatting a table involves changing the appearance of the text and adding borders and shading. Be careful to select the exact cells that you want to format before using the commands described in this task, and remember that you can always use Undo if you make a change you don't like. To learn more ways to format a table, see "Enhancing Your Table" later in Part 9.

✓ **Adding shading to cells**

If you want to add shading to some of the cells in your table, select the cells, and then choose **Format, Borders and Shading**. Click the **Shading** tab, click the color you'd like to use, and click **OK**.

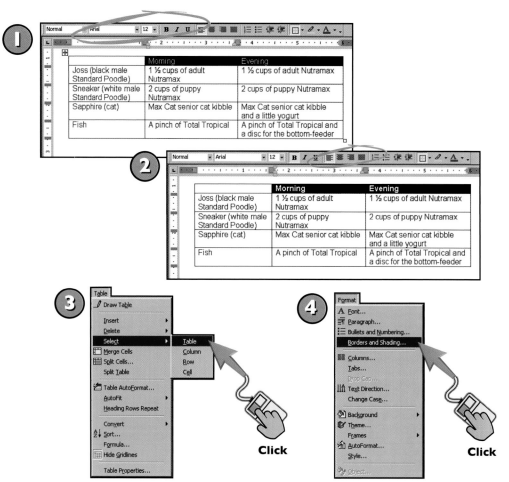

1. To change text formatting, select the cells (or some text within a cell) and then use the familiar drop-down lists and buttons in the Formatting toolbar.

2. To change the alignment of text within cells, select the cells and then click desired alignment button on the Formatting toolbar.

3. To change the border around the outside of the table, first select the entire table by choosing **Table**, **Select**, **Table**.

4. Next, choose **Format**, **Borders and Shading**.

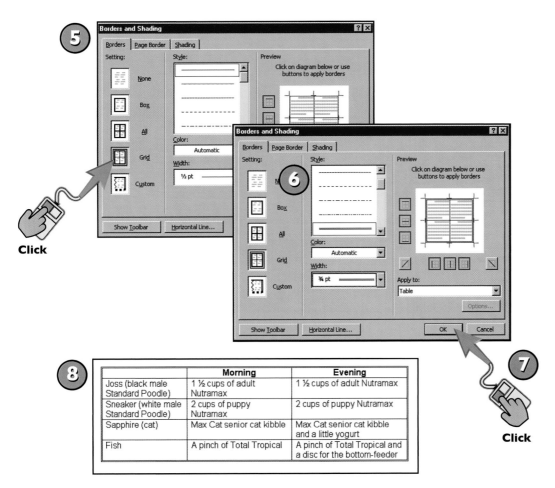

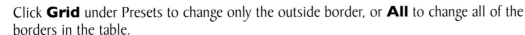

**Moving and resizing a table**

To move your table around on the page, use the small square that contains a four-headed arrow, located just outside the upper-left corner of the table (see the figure for step 1). Point to this square and drag the table to the desired location. To resize your table, point to the small square just outside the lower-right corner, and drag diagonally up and to the left to shrink the table, or down and to the right to enlarge it.

(5) Click **Grid** under Presets to change only the outside border, or **All** to change all of the borders in the table.

(6) Choose the desired options from the **Style**, **Color**, and **Width** lists.

(7) Click the **OK** button.

(8) Word applies the border options you chose.

End Task

# Task 7: Drawing a Table

## Using the Tables and Borders Toolbar

If you want to make a complex table, you'll probably find it easier to "draw" the table with your mouse than to use the Insert Table toolbar button. In this task, you use the **Draw Table** button on the Tables and Borders toolbar to draw the outside border of a table and then fill in the rows and columns. This method of creating a table is extremely flexible; if you can envision a design for your table, you can almost certainly create it.

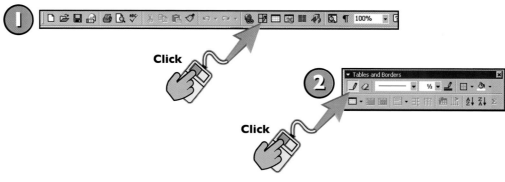

Click

Click

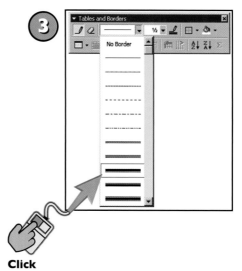

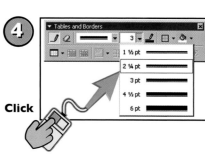

Click

Click

✓ **Changing the appearance of a line**
To change the appearance of a line after you've already drawn it, select the desired options in the **Line Style, Line Weight,** and **Border Color** lists in the Tables and Borders toolbar, and draw over the line again with Draw Table tool.

1️⃣ Click the **Tables and Borders** button on the Standard toolbar.

2️⃣ Click the **Draw Table** button if it isn't already selected (pushed in). Your mouse pointer will now look like a small pencil when it's over your document.

3️⃣ Display the **Line Style** drop-down list and choose a line style for the outside border of your table.

4️⃣ Display the **Line Weight** drop-down list and choose a line weight for the outside border of your table.

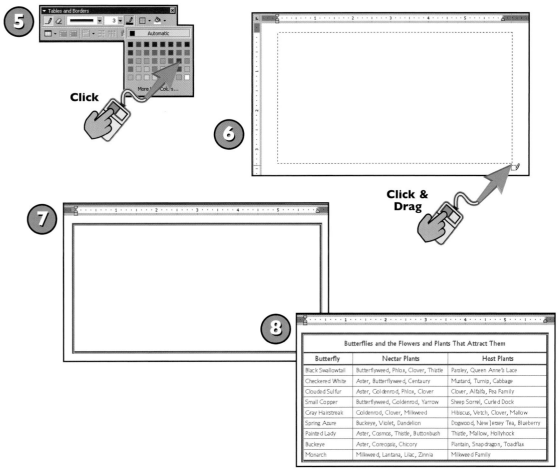

**Click**

**Click &
Drag**

Butterflies and the Flowers and Plants That Attract Them

| Butterfly | Nectar Plants | Host Plants |
|---|---|---|
| Black Swallowtail | Butterflyweed, Phlox, Clover, Thistle | Parsley, Queen Anne's Lace |
| Checkered White | Aster, Butterflyweed, Centaury | Mustard, Turnip, Cabbage |
| Clouded Sulfur | Aster, Goldenrod, Phlox, Clover | Clover, Alfalfa, Pea Family |
| Small Copper | Butterflyweed, Goldenrod, Yarrow | Sheep Sorrel, Curled Dock |
| Gray Hairstreak | Goldenrod, Clover, Milkweed | Hibiscus, Vetch, Clover, Mallow |
| Spring Azure | Buckeye, Violet, Dandelion | Dogwood, New Jersey Tea, Blueberry |
| Painted Lady | Aster, Cosmos, Thistle, Buttonbush | Thistle, Mallow, Hollyhock |
| Buckeye | Aster, Coreopsis, Chicory | Plantain, Snapdragon, Toadflax |
| Monarch | Milkweed, Lantana, Lilac, Zinnia | Milkweed Family |

**5** Click the **Border Color** button and click a color for the outside border of your table.

**6** Starting in the upper-left corner, drag diagonally down and to the right, and release the mouse button when the outline is the right size.

**7** Word creates the outside border of your table. Now repeat steps 3 through 5 to choose what kind of lines you want, and draw the internal lines in the table.

**8** Click the **Draw Table** button to turn it off, and enter the text in the table. For tips on improving the appearance of the text in your table, see next task.

**Hiding lines**
To hide a line in a table, first display the Line Style list and choose the **No Border** option. Then click the **Draw Table** button and drag over the line. If you want to actually *remove* a line, merging the cells that were on either side of it, see the next task.

# Task 8: Enhancing Your Table

## Improving Your Table's Appearance

**Regardless of whether you create your table with the Insert Table button or you draw it with the Draw Table button, you can easily adjust the table and the text it contains with tools in the Tables and Borders toolbar. In this task, you first learn how to select a single cell or group of cells—an essential part of formatting cells in your table—and then you practice using some of the most useful of tools in the Tables and Borders toolbar.**

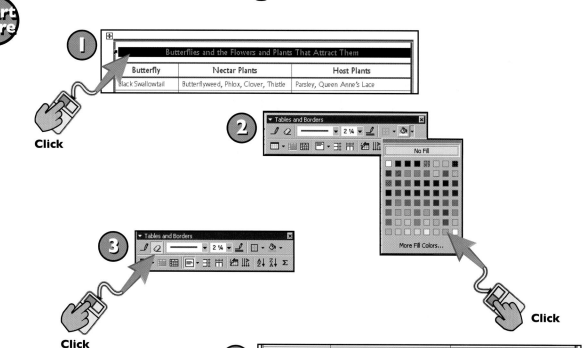

Start Here

Click

Click

Click

Click & Drag

1. To select a cell, point just inside the left edge of the cell. When the mouse pointer becomes a black arrow, click once (or drag to select multiple cells).

2. To add shading to a cell, select the cell, click the **down arrow** to the right of the **Shading Color** button on the Tables and Borders toolbar, and click the desired color.

3. To remove a line in a table and merge the cells on either side of the line, first click the **Eraser** button.

4. The mouse pointer becomes an eraser. Drag over the line to highlight it, and then release the mouse button.

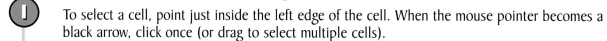

Next Step

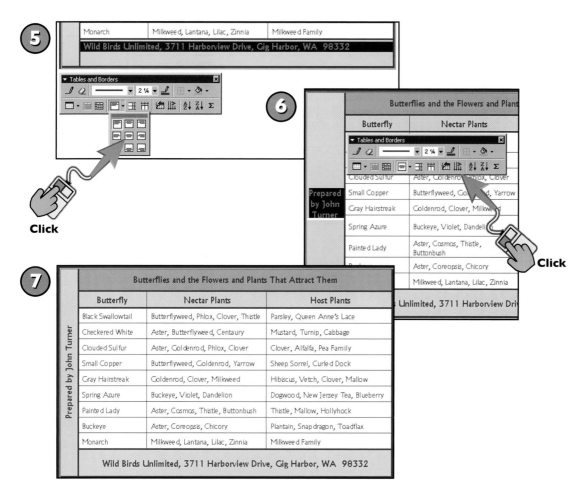

**Click**

**Click**

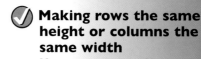

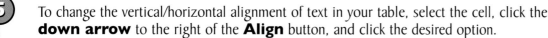

**5** To change the vertical/horizontal alignment of text in your table, select the cell, click the **down arrow** to the right of the **Align** button, and click the desired option.

**6** To change the direction of text from left-to-right to either bottom-to-top or top-to-bottom, select the cell and then click the **Change Text Direction** button one or more times.

**7** Make any further adjustments to your table until you're satisfied with its appearance.

✅ **Making rows the same height or columns the same width**
If you want to make multiple rows the same height or multiple columns the same width, select the rows or columns (see steps 2 and 4 of "Adding, Deleting, and Resizing Rows and Columns" previously in Part 9), and then click the **Distribute Rows Evenly** or **Distribute Columns Evenly** button on the Tables and Borders toolbar.

End
Task

# Adding Graphics to Your Document

Working with graphics used to be out of reach for almost everyone but professional graphic designers. Now it takes only a click or two to spice up a document with a splashy graphic or a colorful title. In this part, you learn how to insert, manipulate, and format graphic images, how to adjust the way text flows around an image, and how to use WordArt, a wonderful tool that lets you create special effects for text.

# Tasks

10

## Adding Graphics to Your Document

Adding a graphic to your document is not as hard as you might think. In fact, it only takes a click or two. This task describes how to insert clip art images contained on the **Microsoft Office (or Word) CD,** although you can certainly use other image files— photographs or images that you've scanned, drawings that you've created in other programs, and so on—and the files can be located in any folder on your computer system. After you've added a graphic to your document, you'll want to look over the next three tasks to learn how to adjust its location and appearance, among other things.

# Task 1: Inserting a Graphic in Your Document

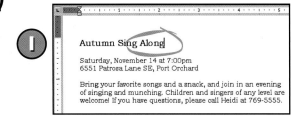

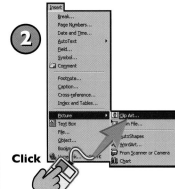

Click

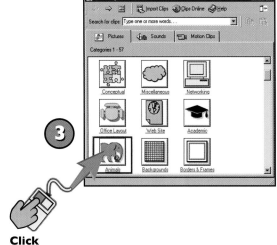

**Click**

**Click**

**Click**

1. Move the insertion point to the approximate place where you want to insert the graphic.

2. Place the Microsoft Office (or Word) CD in your CD-ROM drive, and choose **Insert**, **Picture**, **Clip Art** to display the Insert ClipArt dialog box.

3. In the **Pictures** tab, scroll through the categories of images and click one that you'd like to browse.

4. To return to the list of categories, click the **All Categories** button.

 Page **174**

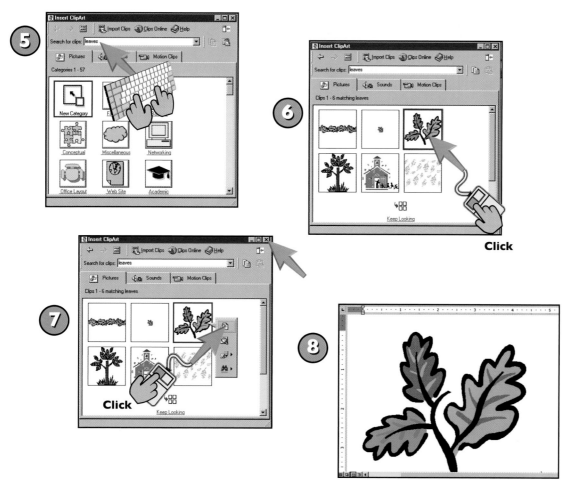

**Click**

**Click**

✅ **Using a graphic located on your hard disk**

If you want to insert a graphic from a folder on your hard disk instead of from the Microsoft Office CD, choose **Insert, Picture, From File**. In the Insert Picture dialog box, select the desired graphics file and click the **Insert** button.

✅ **Looking for clip art at the Microsoft Web site**

If you don't find a suitable clip art image in the Insert ClipArt dialog box, you can click the **Clips Online** button at the top of the dialog box to connect to Microsoft's Clip Gallery Live Web site. (If you are not already connected to the Internet, you will be prompted to connect.) At this site, you can browse Microsoft's collection of images and download them for free.

⑤ If you know what type of image you're looking for, type a descriptive word or two in the **Search for clips** box, and press **Enter**.

⑥ Word displays the images that most closely match your keywords. When you find an image that you want to use, click it to display a small toolbar.

⑦ Click the **Insert Clip** button to insert the image in your document, and then click the **Close** button in upper-right corner of Insert ClipArt dialog box.

⑧ The graphic is inserted in your document. Don't worry if it is not the right size. You'll learn how to resize it in the next task.

# Task 2: Moving and Sizing a Graphic

## Changing the Size and Location of a Graphic in Your Document

After you've placed a graphic in your document, you need to adjust its size and move it to the correct place. By default, Word places images *in-line*, meaning that they are in the same "layer" of the document as the text. You can resize an image when it's in-line. However, if you want to move an image, it's easier if the image is not in-line. As you'll learn in this task, the best way to make this change is to set a *text wrapping* option. (You'll learn more about text wrapping options in "Controlling the Text Flow Around a Graphic" later in Part 10.)

Start Here

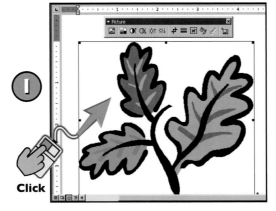
① Click

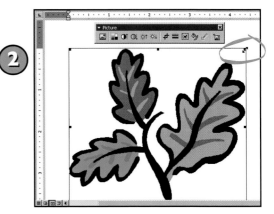
②

③ Click & Drag

Autumn Sing Along
Saturday, November 14 at 7:00pm
6551 Patrosa Lane SE, Port Orchard

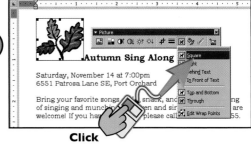
④ Click

Autumn Sing Along
Saturday, November 14 at 7:00pm
6551 Patrosa Lane SE, Port Orchard

Bring your favorite songs and snack, and ... ing
of singing and munch... en and sir... are
welcome! If you hav... please call ...55.

① Click the graphic to select it. When a graphic is selected, small squares (called **selection handles**) appear around the image. When the image is in-line, the squares are black.

② To resize the graphic, point to a corner selection handle (the mouse pointer becomes a diagonal double-headed arrow).

③ Drag to enlarge or shrink the image, and release the mouse button when the image is the correct size.

④ To move a graphic, make sure it's selected, click the **Text Wrapping** button in the Picture toolbar, and click **Square**. (You can always choose a different option later.)

Next Step

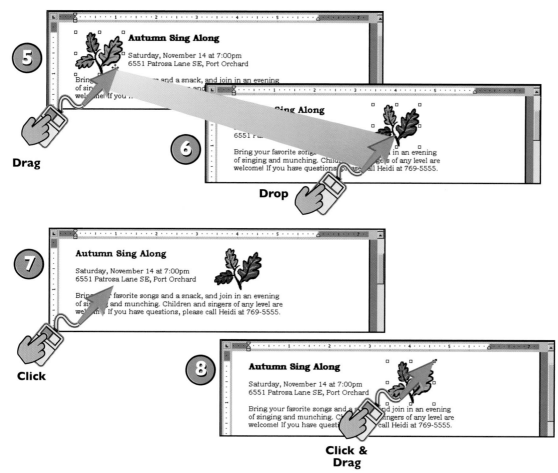

**Drag**

**Drop**

**Click**

**Click & Drag**

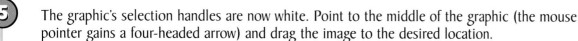

5. The graphic's selection handles are now white. Point to the middle of the graphic (the mouse pointer gains a four-headed arrow) and drag the image to the desired location.

6. Release the mouse button when the image is in the desired place.

7. Click outside of the image to deselect it. This makes it easier to see how the image looks in its new location.

8. When a graphic has white selection handles, you can resize it in exactly the same way as you do when it's in-line: Point to a corner handle and drag in the desired direction.

✓ **Placing a graphic on the left margin, in the center, or at the right margin**
To position graphic precisely on left margin, in the horizontal center of page, or at the right margin, select the graphic (after you've set a text wrapping option) and then double-click it to display the **Format Picture** dialog box. Click **Layout** tab, mark the **Left, Center,** or **Right** option button under **Horizontal alignment,** and click **OK.**

✓ **Displaying the Picture toolbar**
If you don't see the Picture toolbar in step 4, choose **View, Toolbars, Picture.**

End Task

Page
**177**

## Cropping a Graphic and Working with Borders

Word enables you to format graphics in a wide variety of ways. In this task, you learn two techniques to get you started: cropping and adding or removing borders. You crop an image to remove a portion of it (the image's size and proportions remain unchanged). Adding borders around the outside of an image gives it definition, while removing borders makes it blend into the surrounding text. This task assumes your graphic is no longer in-line. If it is still in-line, click it and choose a text-wrapping option to take it "out of line" before continuing with these steps.

# Task 3: Cropping a Graphic and Adding Borders

Click

Click & Drag

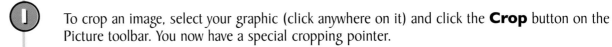

**1** To crop an image, select your graphic (click anywhere on it) and click the **Crop** button on the Picture toolbar. You now have a special cropping pointer.

**2** Drag a selection handle and release the mouse button when the desired portion is cropped out.

**3** In this example, the lower part of the image is cropped out. Click the **Crop** button again to turn it off.

Next Step

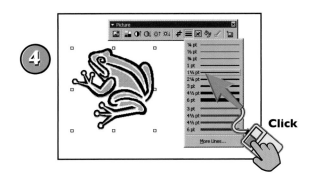

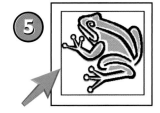

**Click**

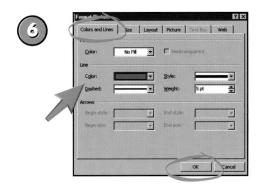

✓ **Displaying the Picture toolbar**
If you don't see the Picture toolbar, choose **View, Toolbars, Picture,** or right-click the graphic and choose **Show Picture Toolbar** in the context menu that appears.

✓ **Removing a border**
To remove a border, double-click the image to display the Format Picture dialog box, click the **Colors and Lines** tab, display the **Color** drop-down list under **Line,** choose **No Line,** and then click **OK**.

④ To add a border to an image, make sure it's selected, and click the **Line Style** button in the Picture toolbar. Choose a line style from the menu that appears.

⑤ Word adds a border to the image. You may want to deselect the image so that you can see the border more clearly.

⑥ To adjust the border's appearance, double-click the image to display the **Format Picture** dialog box, click the **Colors and Lines** tab, choose the desired settings under **Line,** and click **OK**.

⑦ Word modifies the border. (Again, you may want to deselect the image to see the border more clearly.)

## Task 4: Controlling Text Flow Around a Graphic

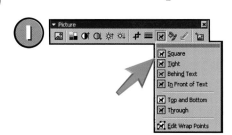

### Setting Text-Wrapping Options

Word gives you several options for controlling how text flows around your graphic image. In this task, you see examples of the five most common text wrapping options. Keep in mind that you can always drag an image around your document regardless of the text wrapping option you choose. (See "Moving and Sizing a Graphic" earlier in Part 10.)

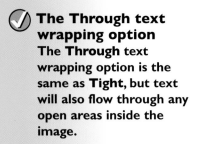

**The Through text wrapping option**
The **Through** text wrapping option is the same as **Tight**, but text will also flow through any open areas inside the image.

**1** To change the way text wraps around your image, select the image, click the **Text Wrapping** button on the Picture toolbar, and click one of the options in the drop-down list.

**2** The **Square** option wraps the text in a square shape around the image.

**3** The **Tight** option wraps the text right up to the outside edges of the image.

### Red Dragon Taichi

Taichi is an internal martial art founded in China. It is called an "internal" martial art because its training focuses on relaxation, alignment, and energy cultivation instead of strength training and athletic conditioning. You can think of Taichi as a moving form of yoga and meditation combined. The movements are performed smoothly, softly, and gracefully. A new 8-week beginning class is starting on November 9. The class meets Mondays and Wednesdays from 5:30p.m. to 7:00p.m., and the cost is $22.50 per month. The instructor, Roger Cloutier, has been practicing Taichi for 29 years and has extensive teaching experience. Classes are easygoing and fun. For more information, call the Givens Community Center at 337-5733.

### Red Dragon Taichi

Taichi is an internal martial art founded in China. It is called an "internal" martial art because its training focuses on relaxation, alignment, and energy cultivation instead of strength training and athletic conditioning. You can think of Taichi as a moving form of yoga and meditation combined. The movements are performed smoothly, softly, and gracefully. A new 8-week beginning class is starting on November 9. The class meets Mondays and Wednesdays from 5:30p.m. to 7:00p.m., and the cost is $22.50 per month. The instructor, Roger Cloutier, has been practicing Taichi for 29 years and has extensive teaching experience. Classes are easygoing and fun. For more information, call the Givens Community Center at 337-5733.

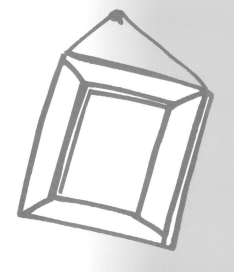

### Red Dragon Taichi

Taichi is an internal martial art founded in China. It is called an "internal" martial art because its training focuses on relaxation, alignment, and energy cul-

tivation instead of strength training and athletic conditioning. You can think of Taichi as a moving form of yoga and meditation combined. The movements are performed smoothly, softly, and gracefully. A new 8-week beginning class is starting on November 9. The class meets Mondays and Wednesdays from 5:30p.m. to 7:00p.m., and the cost is $22.50 per month. The instructor, Roger

 The **Behind Text** option does not wrap the text at all; the image is sent behind the text so that the text flows over the image.

 The **In Front of Text** option also doesn't wrap the text; the image appears in front of the text so that the text is not visible behind it.

 The **Top and Bottom** option wraps the text above and below the image, but not along its sides.

# Task 5: Adding Shapes

## Adding Shapes to Your Document

Sometimes you don't need a complex graphic in your document—just something simple, such as an arrow or a box. Word's AutoShapes feature enables you to quickly draw arrows, rectangles, ovals, callouts, banners, and so on. After you have inserted a shape, you can use many of the same methods you learned in the last two tasks to move and resize it, modify its borders, and so on. In this task, you add a shape to a document and then change its fill color.

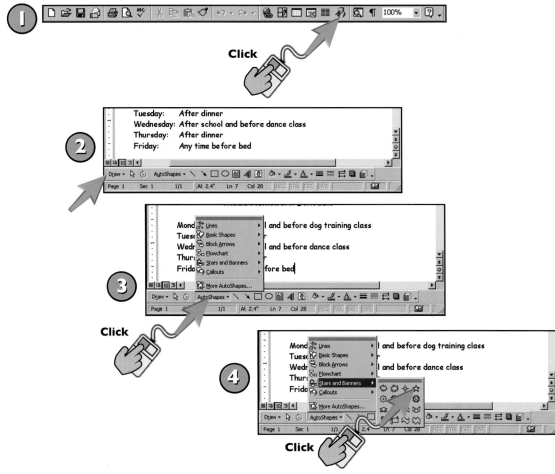

Click

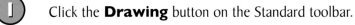

1. Click the **Drawing** button on the Standard toolbar.

2. The Drawing toolbar appears by default at the bottom of the Word window.

3. Click the **AutoShapes** button to display a menu with categories of AutoShapes.

4. Point to a category, and then click the desired shape in the submenu that appears.

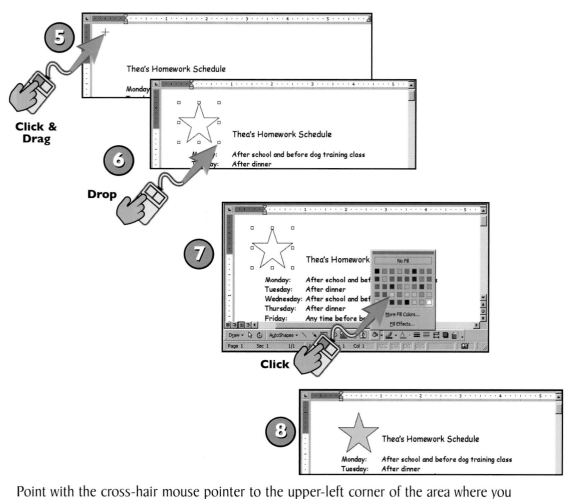

Click &
Drag

Drop

Click

**5** Point with the cross-hair mouse pointer to the upper-left corner of the area where you want to draw the shape, and drag diagonally down and to the right.

**6** Release the mouse button to finish drawing the shape.

**7** Keep the shape selected, click the **down arrow** to the right of the **Fill Color** button in the Drawing toolbar, and click a color.

**8** The shape takes on the fill color you chose. (Deselect the shape to see it more clearly.)

✔ **Creating a perfect shape**
If you are using the rectangle shape and want to draw a perfect square, hold down the **Shift** key as you drag. This also works with the oval shape to get a perfect circle, the star shape to get a perfectly proportioned star, and so on.

✔ **Deleting a shape**
If you don't like a shape that you drew, just click it to select it and then press the Delete key.

End
Task

# Task 6: Creating WordArt

When you add graphics to a document, you aren't limited to working with images separate from your text. WordArt lets you add flair to your text itself. It's perfect for creating splashy headings and titles. You start with a basic "look" for your word or phrase, and then tweak it to get the exact effect you want. Once you've added a WordArt image, you can use the techniques described earlier in this part to move or resize it, or to add borders.

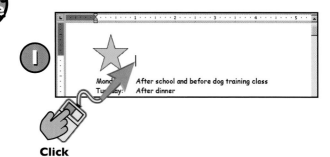

Click

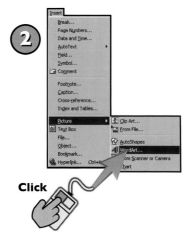

Click

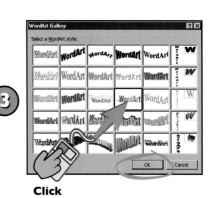

Click

**✓ Modifying a WordArt image**
To revise the WordArt text or change its appearance after you've created the image, use the WordArt toolbar. This toolbar appears as soon as you insert a WordArt image. If you don't see it, choose **View, Toolbars, WordArt**.

① Click where you want the WordArt image to go.

② Choose **Insert**, **Picture**, **WordArt**. (If your Drawing toolbar is displayed, you can also click the Insert WordArt button on this toolbar.)

③ The WordArt Gallery dialog box opens. Click the look you want to start with, and click the **OK** button.

④ The Edit WordArt Text window appears.

Next Step

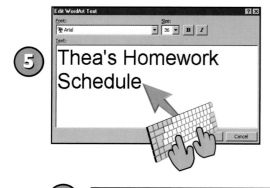

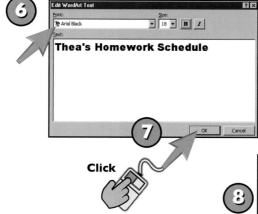

**Click**

(5) Type the text for your WordArt image, replacing the *Your Text Here* dummy text. (The text won't take on the look you chose in step 3 until it's inserted in your document.)

(6) Use the **Font** and **Size** drop-down lists and the **Bold** and **Italic** buttons to make additional adjustments to the text.

(7) Click the **OK** button.

(8) The WordArt image is inserted in your document.

# Mass Mailings

Mail merge automates the process of inserting personal information, such as names and addresses, into a document that you want to send to many people. You can use it to create such documents as personalized form letters for a mass mailing, cover letters for a batch of résumés, or marketing letters for publicity packages. Not only that, you can also use mail merge to print envelopes or labels to go with your letters. You should follow the steps in the first five tasks in of this part (from "Starting the Main Document" to "Merging the Documents") in sequence. Each task picks up where the previous one left off. Once you've run through these five tasks a time or two, you'll have no problem following the instructions in the last two tasks to merge your envelopes or labels.

# Tasks

## Starting the Main Document

In this first phase of the mail merge process, you simply tell Word which document you want to use as the *main document*. You can either open an existing main document or start a new one. If you start a new one, as described in these steps, you don't have to type any of the document now; you simply save a blank document. In "Completing the Main Document" later in Part 11, you come back to the main document and enter both regular text and special *merge fields* telling Word where to insert each piece of information from the data source.

# Task 1: Starting the Main Document

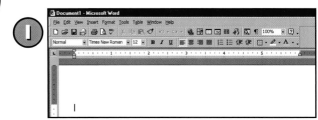

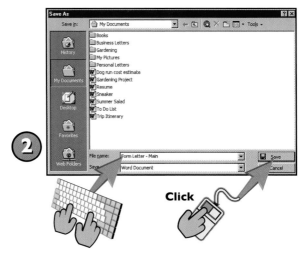

Click

Click

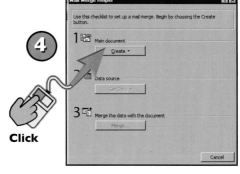

Click

Click

1. Start a new, blank document in Word (see "Creating a New Document" in Part 4).

2. Save the document with a name such as **Form Letter - Main** to remind you that it's a main document (see "Saving a Document" in Part 4).

3. Choose **Tools**, **Mail Merge** to display the Mail Merge Helper dialog box.

4. Click the **Create** button.

Next Step

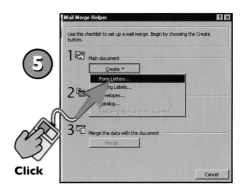

**Click**

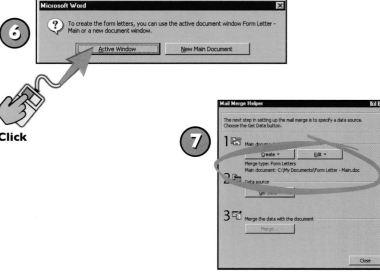

**Click**

(5) Click **Form Letters** in the **Create** drop-down list.

(6) A message box appears. Click the **Active Window** button to tell Word that your main document is already open.

(7) The Mail Merge Helper dialog box appears again with information about the main document. Continue with the next task.

# Creating the Data Source for the Mail Merge

In this second phase of the mail merge process, you tell Word which document you want to use as your *data source*. You can either create a new one or open an existing one. You learn how to create a new one here. In "Merging Envelopes" and "Merging Labels" later in Part 11, you learn how to open an existing data source. The key step in creating a data source is telling Word which *fields*, or pieces of information, you want to store. Typical fields are first name, last name, company, address, city, state, zip code, and so on.

# Task 2: Creating and Saving the Data Source

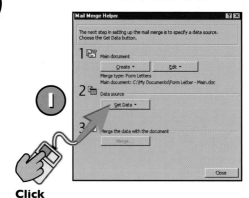

**Click**

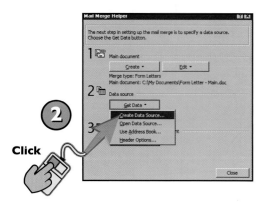

**Click**

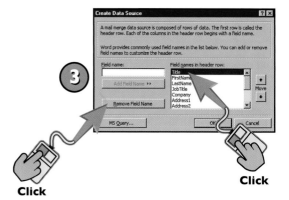

**Click**

**Click**

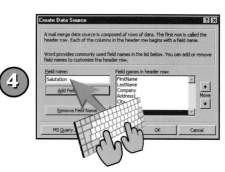

**Click**

1. Click the **Get Data** button in the Mail Merge Helper dialog box, left open from the previous task.

2. Choose **Create Data Source** in the **Get Data** drop-down list to display the Create Data Source dialog box.

3. To remove a field that you don't want, click it in the **Field names in header row** list and click the **Remove Field Name** button.

4. To add a field, first replace the contents of the **Field name** text box with the name of the field you want to add.

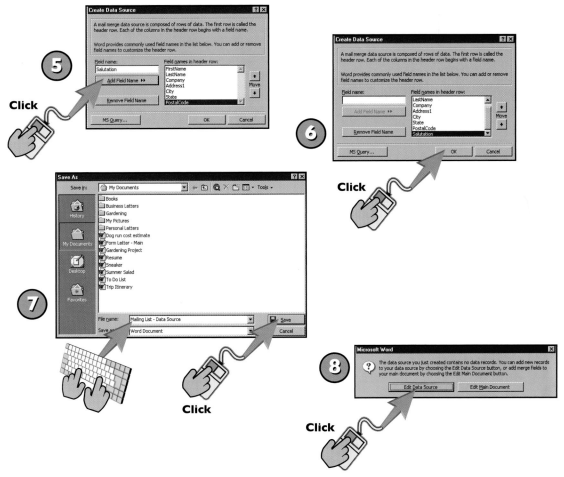

**5**    Then click the **Add Field Name** button to add the name to the **Field names in header row** list.

**6**    When your list of fields is the way you want it, click **OK**.

**7**    Word displays the Save As dialog box. Save your data source with a name such as **Mailing List - Data Source**.

**8**    When Word asks what you want to do next, click the **Edit Data Source** button and continue with the next task.

## Adding Records to the Data Source

In this third phase of the mail merge process, you enter data into your data source. The data for each person is called a *record*. When you merge the documents later, Word will merge the information from each record into the main document to create your personalized form letters (or envelopes or labels).

✓ **Editing your data source**

The easiest way to edit your data source in the future is to open it *through* the main document. First open the main document. Then click the **Edit Data Source** button at the far right end of the Mail Merge toolbar (see the next task) to display the Data Form. Edit the records, and then click **OK**. Save the main document, and click **Yes** when Word asks if you want to save the data source.

# Task 3: Entering Records into the Data Source

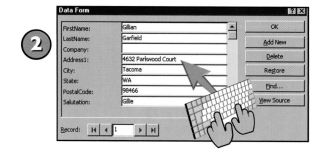

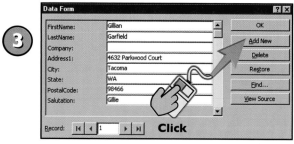

After completing step 8 in the previous task, Word presents a blank Data Form with text boxes for all the fields that you defined in the preceding task.

Enter the information for the first person in your mailing list, using the **Tab** key to move from field to field.

Click the **Add New** button to add the next record. (Be careful not to click the **OK** button at this point.)

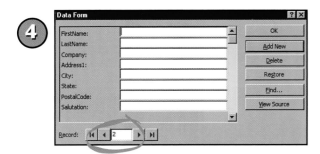

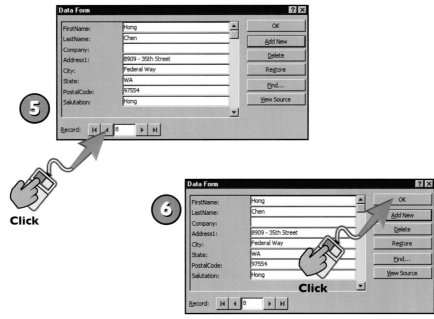

**Click**

**Click**

(4) Word clears the Data Form to let you enter the next record. Continue entering records.

(5) The **Record** arrows let you move forward and back in your data source so that you can edit records you've already entered.

(6) When you've finished entering all the records, click the **OK** button.

## Finishing the Main Document

In this fourth phase of the mail merge process, you finish the main document. This entails typing and formatting the text, and inserting the merge fields that tell Word where to insert the data from your data source.

Start Here

# Task 4: Completing the Main Document

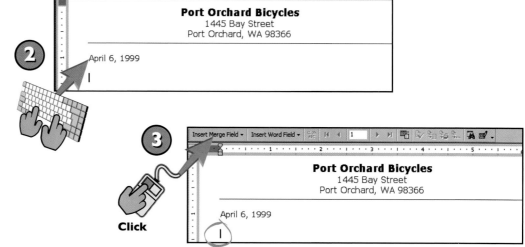

**⚠ Warning**

When you close the main document (either before or after performing the merge), Word may ask if you want to save the data source attached to the main document. If you see this message, click the **Yes** button! Otherwise, any changes you've made to records in your data source won't be saved.

**①** After completing step 6 in the previous task, Word displays your main document. Notice the Mail Merge toolbar that appears directly under the Formatting toolbar.

**②** Type and format the text you want to include above the recipient's address.

**③** Place the insertion point on the first line of the address block, and click the **Insert Merge Field** button in the Mail Merge toolbar.

**④** In the drop-down list that appears, click the first field in the address block.

Next Step

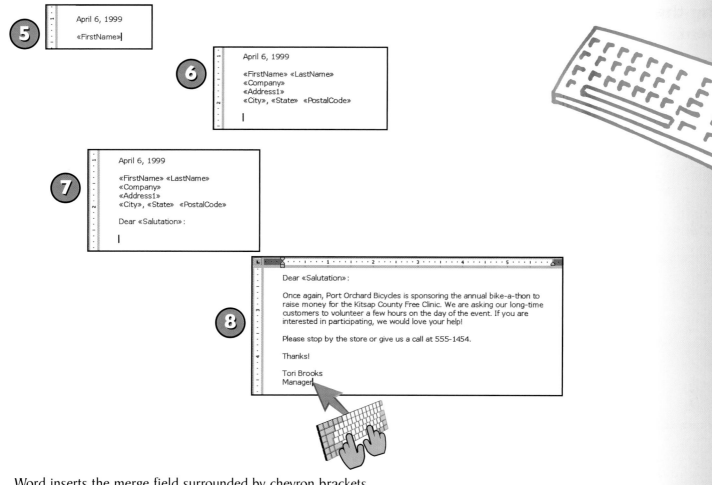

April 6, 1999

«FirstName»

April 6, 1999

«FirstName» «LastName»
«Company»
«Address1»
«City», «State» «PostalCode»

April 6, 1999

«FirstName» «LastName»
«Company»
«Address1»
«City», «State» «PostalCode»

Dear «Salutation»:

Dear «Salutation»:

Once again, Port Orchard Bicycles is sponsoring the annual bike-a-thon to raise money for the Kitsap County Free Clinic. We are asking our long-time customers to volunteer a few hours on the day of the event. If you are interested in participating, we would love your help!

Please stop by the store or give us a call at 555-1454.

Thanks!

Tori Brooks
Manager

**5** Word inserts the merge field surrounded by chevron brackets.

**6** Insert the remaining merge fields in the address block, pressing **Enter** and adding spaces and commas where necessary.

**7** If you have a salutation field, add it after **Dear**, and follow it with a colon or comma.

**8** Type the remaining text and then save the main document. Leave it open for the next task.

# Task 5: Merging the Documents

## Producing the Form Letters

In this final phase of the mail merge process, you merge the main document with the data source to produce your form letters. In these steps, you first check to see if the data will merge correctly, and then merge the letters to a new document window and print them.

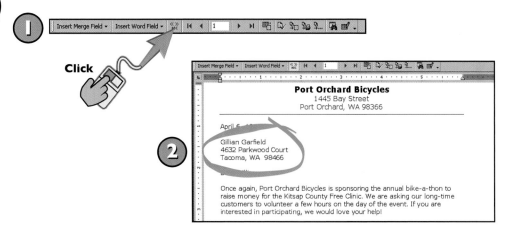

**Click**

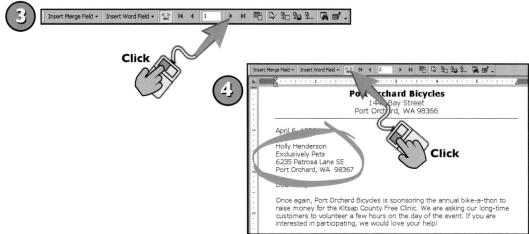

**Click**

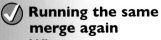

**Running the same merge again**

When you want to merge the same main document and data source in the future, just open the main document and follow steps 5 and 6 in this task.

**1** After completing step 8 in the previous task, click the **View Merged Data** button on the Mail Merge toolbar.

**2** Word displays the data from the first record.

**3** Click the **Next Record** button on the Mail Merge toolbar.

**4** Word displays the data from the next record. Click the **View Merged Data** button again to turn it off.

**Click**

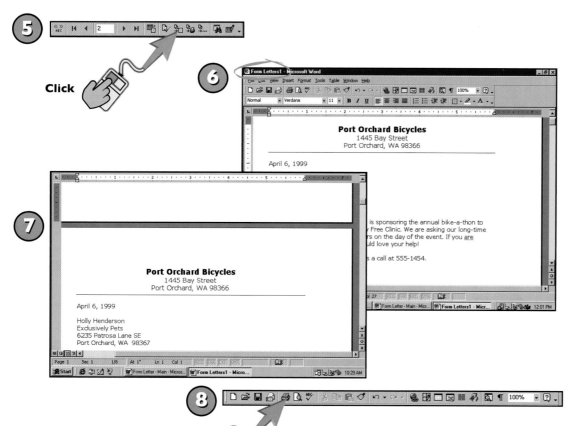

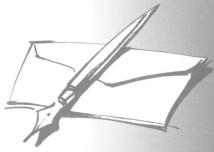

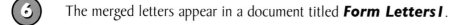

**Click**

**5** Click the **Merge to New Document** button on the Mail Merge toolbar to merge the documents.

**6** The merged letters appear in a document titled **Form Letters1**.

**7** Scroll down the document. The letters print on separate pages because Word separates them with **next page section breaks**.

**8** Click the **Print** button in the Standard toolbar to print the form letters, and then close the document without saving it.

End Task

## Printing Envelopes Using Mail Merge

The general steps for merging envelopes and labels are the same as for merging form letters (although the details are somewhat different). Consequently, you'll find it helpful to practice a few mail merges with form letters before proceeding with this task and the next. Also note that both of these tasks assume you already have a data source, so you'll open an existing one rather than creating a new one.

✓ **Choosing a different envelope size**
If you aren't using standard business envelopes, choose the appropriate envelope size in the **Envelope size** drop-down list in the **Envelope Options** dialog box before clicking OK in step 5.

# Task 6: Merging Envelopes

Start Here

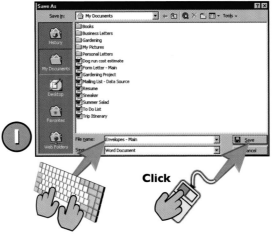

Click

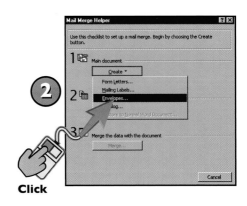

Click

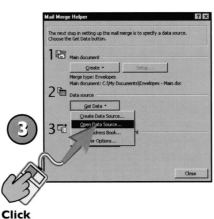

Click

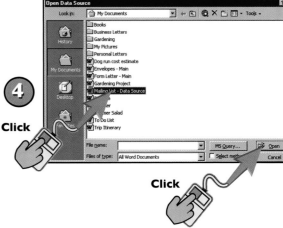

Click

Click

(1) Start a new document and save it with a name such as **Envelopes - Main**.

(2) Choose **Tools, Mail Merge**, click the **Create** button, and click **Envelopes**.

(3) Click the **Active Window** button (not shown), and then click the **Get Data** button in the Mail Merge Helper dialog box and choose **Open Data Source**.

(4) Select your data source in the Open Data Source dialog box, and click the **Open** button.

Next Step

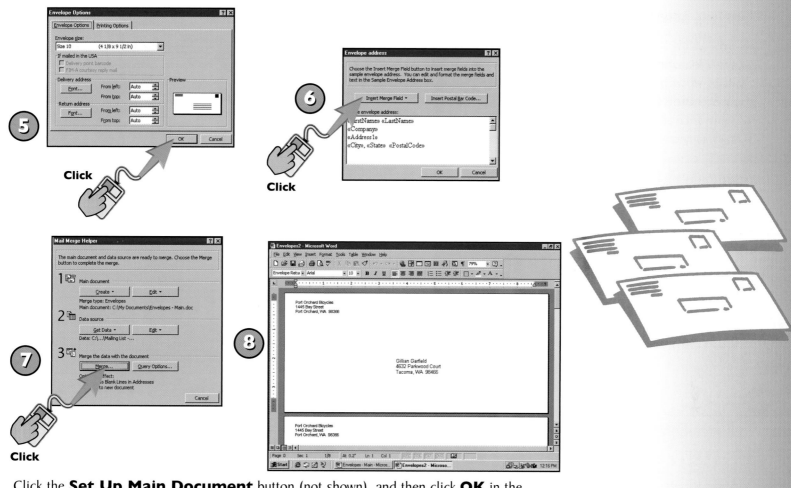

**Click**

**Click**

**Click**

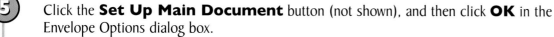

5 Click the **Set Up Main Document** button (not shown), and then click **OK** in the Envelope Options dialog box.

6 Word displays the Envelope Address dialog box. Use the **Insert Merge Field** button to insert the merge fields that you want to include on the envelope. Click **OK**.

7 Click the **Merge** button in the Mail Merge Helper dialog box, and then click the **Merge** button in the Merge dialog box (not shown).

8 The merged envelopes appear onscreen. Print the envelopes and close them without saving. Then save and close the main document.

# Task 7: Merging Labels

## Printing Labels Using Mail Merge

As with merging envelopes, it's easiest to merge labels if you practice a few mail merges with form letters first. And remember that this task assumes you already have a data source, so you'll open an existing one rather than creating a new one.

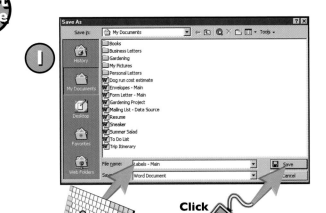

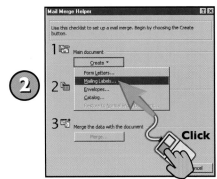

**Click**

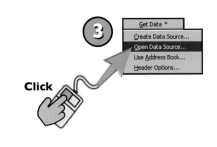

**Click**

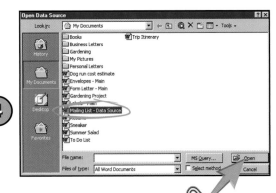

**Click**

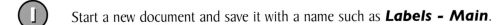

**⊘ Selecting your labels**
If you need help choosing your labels in step 5, see "Printing Labels" in Part 5.

(1) Start a new document and save it with a name such as ***Labels - Main***.

(2) Choose **Tools**, **Mail Merge**, click the **Create** button, and click **Mailing Labels**.

(3) Click the **Active Window** button (not shown), and then click the **Get Data** button in the Mail Merge Helper dialog box and choose **Open Data Source**.

(4) Select your data source in the Open Data Source dialog box, and click the **Open** button.

Next Step

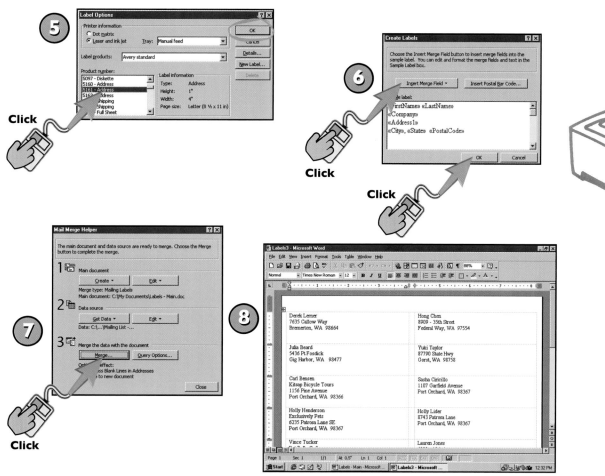

**5** Click the **Set Up Main Document** button (not shown), and then choose the product number for your labels in the Label Options dialog box. Click **OK**.

**6** Word displays the Create Labels dialog box. Use the **Insert Merge Field** button to insert the merge fields that you want to include on your labels. Click **OK**.

**7** Click the **Merge** button in the Mail Merge Helper dialog box, and then click the **Merge** button in the Merge dialog box (not shown).

**8** The merged labels appear onscreen. Print the labels and close them without saving. Then save and close the main document.

End
Task

# Word and the Web

All of the Office 2000 applications, including Word, are designed with Web integration in mind. As we rely increasingly on the Internet in our everyday work, the boundary between documents on our own computers and those on the Web begins to blur. In this part, you learn several ways in which Word's capabilities can augment a company intranet or a Web site on the Internet. You find out how to create links from a Word document to documents on a Web site, how to convert Word documents to Web pages (and vice versa), and how to create Web pages in Word.

# Tasks

# Task 1: Inserting Hyperlinks in a Word Document

## Adding Hyperlinks to Your Word Documents

A *hyperlink* is a "clickable" piece of text or a graphic that leads to another location (the *target* of the hyperlink). With Word's Hyperlink feature, you can create links to other parts of the same document, to other documents, or to Web pages. In this task, you learn how to create a hyperlink to a Web page. Keep in mind that hyperlinks are only useful if your readers will view your Word document onscreen.

✓ **Modifying or removing a hyperlink**
To modify a hyperlink, right-click it and choose **Hyperlink, Edit Hyperlink** to display the Edit Hyperlink dialog box. Click the **ScreenTip** button if you want to change the ScreenTip text (see step 7). Make any other changes to the hyperlink, and click **OK**. To remove a hyperlink, right-click it and choose **Hyperlink, Remove Hyperlink**.

**Start Here**

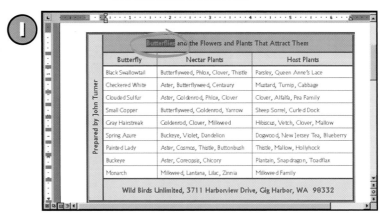

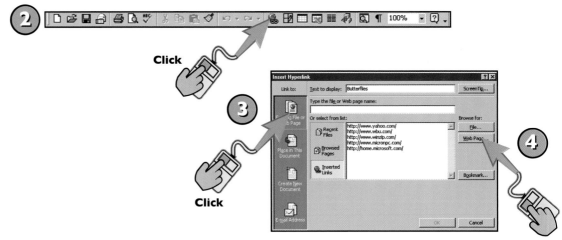

**Click**

**Click**

**Click**

(1) Select the word or phrase that you want to become the hyperlink text.

(2) Click the **Insert Hyperlink** button in the Standard toolbar.

(3) Click the **Existing File or Web Page** button under **Link to**.

(4) Click the **Web Page** button. (Alternatively, you can type the full address of the target Web page in the **Type the file or Web page name** text box and skip to step 6.)

Next Step

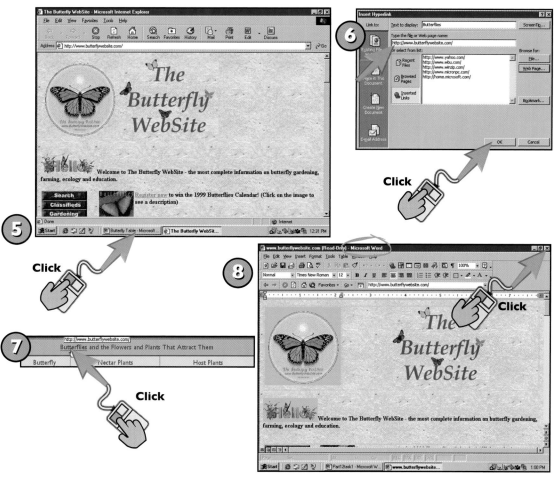

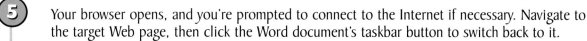

**5** Your browser opens, and you're prompted to connect to the Internet if necessary. Navigate to the target Web page, then click the Word document's taskbar button to switch back to it.

**6** The address of the Web page now appears in the **Type the file or Web page name** text box. Click **OK**.

**7** The hyperlink text is now colored and underlined. When you point to it, the address of the target Web page appears in a ScreenTip. Click the hyperlink.

**8** In a moment, Word displays the target Web page. (You may be prompted to connect to the Internet if you have already disconnected.) When you're finished viewing the page, click the **Close** button.

End Task

**Linking to a document**
To create a link to a document on your network instead of to a Web page, follow steps 1 through 3. Then click the **File** button in the Insert Hyperlink dialog box, select the file in the Link to File dialog box, click **OK**, and click **OK** again.

# Task 2: Converting a Word Document to a Web Page

## Saving a Word Document As a Web Page

If you have information in a Word document you want to make available to others, you can convert the document to a Web page and then post the page on an Internet Web site or a company intranet. Before you convert your document, however, check with your network administrator to see whether it's necessary. In some cases, you can put Word documents on company intranets without changing their format at all.

**✓ Letting other people view your Web pages**
To make your Web pages visible to others, you have to copy (*upload*) them to the Internet or intranet site where they will "live." To do this choose **File**, **Save As**, and then click the **Web Folders**. If you see the location you want, select it and click the **Save** button. If you don't, see the next tip.

**Start Here**

Red Dragon Taichi

Taichi is an internal martial art founded in China. It is called an "internal" martial art because its training focuses on relaxation, alignment, and energy cultivation instead of strength training and athletic conditioning. You can think of Taichi as a moving form of yoga and meditation combined. The movements are performed smoothly, softly, and gracefully. A new 8-week beginning class is starting on November 9. The class meets Mondays and Wednesdays from 5:30p.m. to 7:00p.m., and the cost is $22.50 per month. The instructor, Roger Cloutier, has been practicing Taichi for 29 years and has extensive teaching experience. Classes are easygoing and fun. For more information, call the Givens Community Center at 337-5733.

**Click**

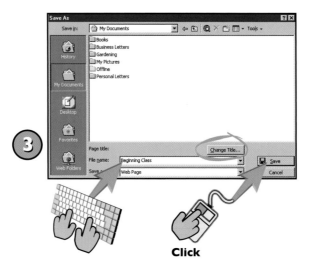

**Click**

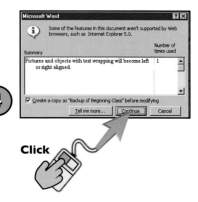

**Click**

**1** Open the Word document you want to convert.

**2** Choose **File**, **Save As Web Page** to display the Save As dialog box.

**3** Optionally, click the **Change Title** button to revise the title that will appear in the title bar for the page. Then specify a name and location for the page, and click the **Save** button.

**4** You may see a message stating how Word will modify formatting that can't be rendered in a Web page. If you do, click the **Continue** button.

Next Step

## Red Dragon Taichi

Taichi is an internal martial art founded in China. It is called an "internal" martial art because its training focuses on relaxation, alignment, and energy cultivation instead of strength training and athletic conditioning. You can think of Taichi as a moving form of yoga and meditation combined. The movements are performed smoothly, softly, and gracefully. A new 8-week beginning class is starting on November 9. The class meets Mondays and Wednesdays from 5:30p.m. to 7:00p.m., and the cost is $22.50 per month. The instructor, Roger Cloutier, has been practicing Taichi for 29 years and has extensive teaching experience. Classes are easygoing and fun. For more information, call the Givens Community Center at 337-5733.

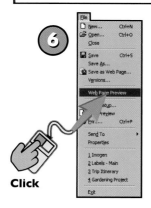

**Click**

**Click**

The newly converted Web page appears in the Word window. Word automatically switches to Web Layout view (**View**, **Web Layout**) whenever it displays a Web page.

If you want to see what the page will look like when viewed in a browser, choose **File**, **Web Page Preview**.

Your browser opens and displays the Web page. Click its **Close** button when you're finished viewing the page.

 **Defining a location for your Web pages**
If you don't have any Web folders defined (see the previous tip), you can specify the location yourself. As a first step, you need to choose **File, Save As**, and then select **Add/Modify FTP Locations** in the **Save in** list to tell Word about your site. (You typically upload pages to a Web or intranet site via a *protocol* called FTP, for file transfer protocol.) From then on, when you want to upload a page, you open it, choose **File, Save As**, select the site under **FTP Locations** in the **Save in** list, select the desired folder at the site, and click the **Save** button. Ask your network administrator for help with the details.

# Task 3: Converting a Web Page to a Word Document

## Saving a Web Page as a Word Document

Once in a while, you may want to save a Web page as a Word document. Perhaps you found a recipe on a Web site and want to edit the text in Word, or you discovered a Web page about woodworking and want to take advantage of Word's formatting and printing capabilities to spruce it up a bit. When you convert a Web page to a Word document, Word does its best to preserve the formatting in the page.

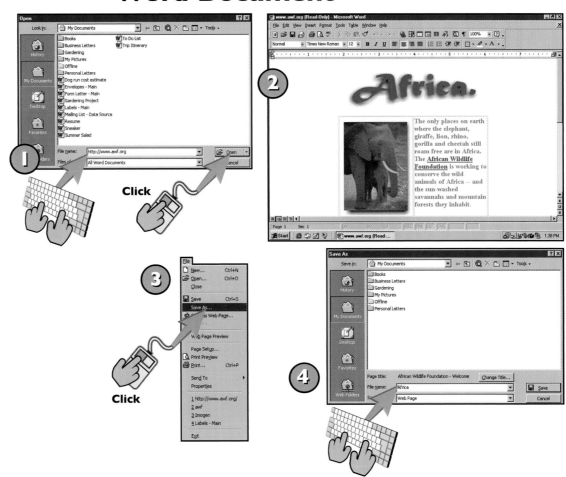

**Click**

**Click**

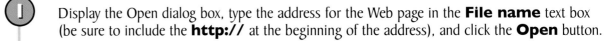

1. Display the Open dialog box, type the address for the Web page in the **File name** text box (be sure to include the **http://** at the beginning of the address), and click the **Open** button.

2. Word prompts you to connect to the Internet if necessary, and then opens the Web page in the Word window.

3. Choose **File**, **Save As** to display the Save As dialog box.

4. Choose a location for the document, and type a name in the **File name** text box.

Next Step

**Click**

**Click**

Display the **Save as type** drop-down list and select **Word Document**.

Click the **Save** button.

The Web page is saved as a Word document.

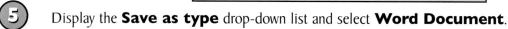

✓ **Another way to open a Web page in Word**
Step 1 describes how to open a Web page directly from the Internet. You could also use your browser to save the page to your hard disk, and then open it from your hard disk. If you use this latter method, be sure to select **All Files** in the **Files of type** list in the Open dialog box so that the Web page will be visible. (By default, Word only shows Word documents in the Open dialog box.)

End Task

# Task 4: Creating a Web Page in Word

## Creating Web Pages

Word gives you a variety of ways to create Web pages—and you don't have to be a professional Web page designer to make them look good. In this task, you get a quick taste of creating a Web page from scratch. For practice, you'll create a "personal Web page" and use one of Word's many *themes* to give the page some visual flair.

(✓) **Working with hyperlinks in Web pages**

You can add hyperlinks to your Web page (or modify existing ones) in the same way that you do with Word documents. See "Inserting Hyperlinks in a Word Document" earlier in Part 12.

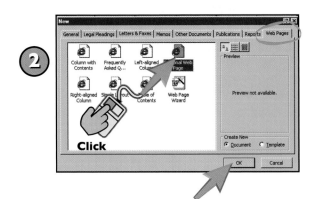

**Click**

**Click**

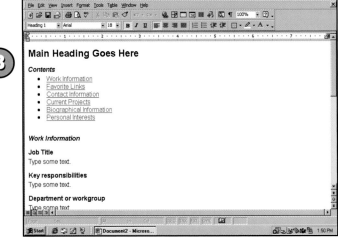

**Click**

 Choose **File**, **New** to display the New dialog box.

 Click the **Web Pages** tab, click the **Personal Web Page** icon, and then click the **OK** button.

 The default Web page opens. The hyperlinks under Contents (Work Information, Favorite Links, and so on) lead to locations in the same page.

 To make the page more visually appealing, choose **Format**, **Theme**.

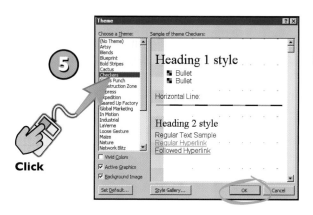

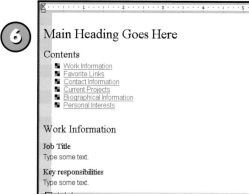

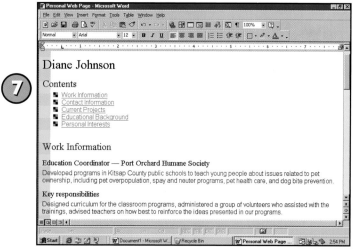

In the Theme dialog box, click a few themes in the **Choose a theme** list. You can preview each theme in the **Sample of theme** area. When you find one that you like, select it and click **OK**.

Word applies the theme to the Web page.

Select all of the "placeholder" text and replace it with your actual text. Then save and close the page.

**Uploading your Web page**
Once you've created a Web page, you have to put it on an internet Web site or on an Intranet where others can access it. For more information, see the tip in "Converting a Word Document to a Web Page" earlier in Part 12.

End Task

**alignment**   The way text aligns along the right and left sides of the page. You can set the alignment of each paragraph in your document.

**alignment, centered**   The text is centered horizontally on the page.

**alignment, justified**   Both the left and right edges of the text are straight. Word adds or removes space between characters to form the straight right edge.

**alignment, left**   The left edge of the text is straight and the right edge is ragged. This is the default alignment option.

**alignment, right**   The right edge of the text is straight and the left edge is ragged.

**AutoCorrect**   A feature that corrects spelling errors as you type. You can also use AutoCorrect to enter long phrases automatically.

**AutoText**   A feature that lets Word "memorize" long blocks of text that you use frequently so that you can quickly insert them in your document.

**cell**   A box in a table, formed by the intersection of a row and a column.

**check box**   A small box that you click to enable or disable an option in a dialog box. If the check box has a check mark in it, the option is currently enabled; if it's clear, the option is disabled. Check boxes are not mutually exclusive; you can mark several check boxes in a group.

**context menu**   A menu that appears when you right-click on something. The commands in a context menu vary depending on where you right-click.

**copy and paste**   To place a duplicate of the selected text somewhere else in the current document or another document.

**cut and paste**   To move the selected text somewhere else in the current document or another document.

**default**   The assumed option, behavior, or formatting that remains in effect unless you specify otherwise.

**dialog box**   A small window that appears when you issue a command followed by ellipses (...) to get more information about how you want to carry out the command. Clicking the OK button in a dialog box issues the command; clicking the Cancel button cancels it.

**docked toolbar**   A toolbar that is fixed on an edge of the Word window.

**drag**   To press and hold down your mouse button as you move the mouse pointer. You typically drag to move, draw, or select objects with the mouse.

**drop-down list**   A list that stays hidden from view until you click the down arrow to its right. As soon as you select an option from the list, the list closes again.

**end mark**   The small horizontal bar at the very end of a Word document. The end mark is only visible in Normal view, and it doesn't print.

**field**   A holding place for information that can be updated. Typical fields in Word include the date field, which displays the current date; and the page number field, which displays the correct page number on each page in a document. *See also* **mail merge, merge field**.

**floating toolbar**   A toolbar that is located somewhere over the Word window, not along one of the edges. A floating toolbar has a title bar, which you can drag to move the toolbar around.

**font**   In the Windows environment, the term *font* refers to a typeface, or character shape, such as Times New Roman or Arial.

**font, printer**   A font that comes with your printer. Printer fonts print correctly, but may not look onscreen exactly as they will when printed.

**font, TrueType**   A font that looks the same onscreen as it does when it prints.

**full menu**   A menu that displays the full set of commands in the menu. If you are using personalized menus, you can click the down arrow at the bottom of a menu to display the full menu. If you are not using personalized menus, you see full menus all of the time. *See also* **short menu**.

**hover**   To rest your mouse pointer over an item for a few moments. Hovering often displays a ScreenTip that identifies the item. *See also* **ScreenTip**.

**I-beam**   The mouse pointer you see when it's resting over text. When you see an I-beam, you can click to move the insertion point, or drag to select text.

**indent**   To push the text in a paragraph in from the margin. Word gives you four indent options (see the next four entries). You can set the indentation of each paragraph in your document.

**indent, first-line**   Only the first line of a paragraph is indented.

**indent, hanging**   All of the lines in a paragraph except the first line are indented.

**indent, left**   All of the lines in a paragraph are indented from the left.

**indent, right**   All of the lines in a paragraph are indented from the right.

**insertion point**   The flashing vertical bar in a document that indicates where text will be inserted or deleted when you type or delete text.

**item** In a general sense, refers to any object on your screen. Also refers to a block of cut or copied text that is stored on the Office Clipboard. *See also* **Office Clipboard**.

**line spacing** The amount of vertical space between lines of text.

**mail merge** The process of merging a "boilerplate" document (such as a form letter, label, or envelope) with a list of data (usually names and addresses) to generate personalized documents.

**mail merge, data source** The file that contains the data you will merge into the "boilerplate" document (called the *main document*). *See also* **mail merge, main document**.

**mail merge, main document** The actual document that you are producing, such as a form letter, label, or envelope.

**mail merge, merge field** Fields that you insert in a main document telling Word where to insert the individual pieces of data (name, address, and so on) from the data source.

**mail merge, record** All of the information about one person in your data source. If you have names and addresses of 50 people in your data source, your data source contains 50 records. Each record is composed of individual fields for the specific pieces of information, such as first name, last name, address, and so on.

**memory** The temporary storage area in your computer that holds the programs and documents that you currently have open (also called RAM, for *random access memory*). Memory is cleared each time you turn off your computer. If you want to return to a document later, you need to save it to disk.

**Office Clipboard** A temporary storage area that holds multiple pieces of cut or copied text. You can paste items in the Office Clipboard into any Office document, in any order.

**option button** A small white circle that you click to choose an option in a dialog box. If the option button has a black dot in it, it is currently enabled; if it doesn't, it is disabled. Option buttons are mutually exclusive; you can only mark one option button in a group.

**orientation, landscape** The document prints so that the long edge of the paper is at the top of the page.

**orientation, portrait** The document prints so that the short edge of the paper is at the top of the page. This is the default setting.

**OverType mode**  When you turn on this feature, each character you type replaces the existing character to the right of the insertion point. By default, OverType mode is turned off, so as you type, existing characters are not replaced; they just move to the right to make room for the new text.

**paragraph mark**  This symbol (¶) indicates the end of a paragraph. A paragraph symbol is inserted each time you press the Enter key. You can see where the paragraph marks in a document are by turning on the Show/Hide button on the Standard toolbar.

**personal menu**  The type of menu that you see when personalized menus are turned on (also called a *short menu*). Word watches how you use the program and only includes in the menus the commands that you use the most frequently.

**Places Bar**  The vertical bar on the left side of the Open and Save As dialog boxes that contain buttons for frequently used folders.

**point**  A unit of measurement for font size. Roughly speaking, the point size of a font measures its vertical height. There are approximately 72 points in a vertical inch. Standard business documents usually use a 10- to 12-point font.

**restore**  To return a window back to the size it was before it was last minimized or maximized.

**ScreenTip**  A small "bubble" that appears when you rest your mouse pointer over a toolbar button or other screen element that identifies the item. Also referred to as a *ToolTip*.

**scroll arrows**  The arrows at either end of a scrollbar that you can click to scroll through your document.

**scroll box**  The small box on a scrollbar that you can drag along the bar to scroll in either direction.

**scrollbar**  A long bar that lets you move through your document with the mouse. Word provides a vertical scrollbar on the right side of the window and a horizontal scrollbar along the bottom of the window.

**select**  To mark text in preparation for performing an action on it. Often called *highlighting*. When you select text, it takes on a black background. When you select a graphic image, **selection handles** appear around its edges.

**selection handles**  Small squares around the edges of a graphical image that indicate the graphic is selected.

**short menu**  A menu that only displays the commands you use the most frequently. When personalized menus are turned on, you see short menus by default. *See also **full menu**.*

**shortcut icon**   An icon that opens a program, folder, or file. A shortcut icon is just a pointer to a program, folder, or file. When you delete a shortcut icon, you don't remove the item to which it points.

**spinner arrows**   Small up and down arrows to the right of a text box. Clicking these arrows increases or decreases the number in the text box.

**status bar**   The bar at the very bottom of the Word window. The status bar contains information such as the current page number, the total number of pages in your document, and so on.

**tab**   This term has several meanings: Many dialog boxes have tabs across the top. Clicking the tabs displays different sets of options. This term also refers to the character that is inserted in your document when you press the Tab key. Finally, the term *tab* refers to a tab stop (see the next seven terms).

**tab, bar**   A custom tab stop that creates a vertical line at the tab stop.

**tab, center**   A custom tab stop that centers text over the tab stop.

**tab, custom**   A tab stop that you insert in a document. When you add a custom tab, all the default tabs to its left disappear.

**tab, decimal**   A custom tab stop that aligns text along the decimal point.

**tab, default**   The tab stops that appear automatically in your document. Default tabs are spaced every half-inch across the document, and they remain in effect unless you insert custom tabs (see *also* **tab, custom**).

**tab, left**   A custom tab stop that left-aligns text at the tab stop. The default tabs are also left tabs.

**tab, right**   A custom tab stop that right-aligns text at the tab stop.

**taskbar**   The bar on the Windows desktop (usually at the bottom of the screen) that contains the Start button at one end and the clock at the other. When a Word document is open, a button for it appears on the taskbar.

**template**   A rough "blueprint" for a document. A template usually contains some combination of formatting and text. Word comes with a wide variety of templates.

**template, Blank Document**   See **template, Normal**.

**template, Normal**   The Normal template (also called the *Blank Document template*) is the default template that Word uses for all new documents unless you specify otherwise. This template contains the formatting for a standard business document (Times New Roman, 12-point font, single spacing, 8.5-by-11 inch paper, and so on).

**text box**   A small box in a dialog box in which you can type text or numbers.

**theme**   A collection of design elements that gives a document or Web page a particular "look." Themes can include background images, fonts, horizontal lines, bullets, and so on.

**title bar**   The bar across the top of a window that lists the name of the program and/or document that's open in the window.

**toggle**   A button or keyboard command that you click or press once to turn an option on and again to turn it off.

**Windows Clipboard**   A temporary storage area for data (text, graphics, and so on) that is being cut or copied. The Windows Clipboard can only hold one cut or copied selection at a time. *See also* **Office Clipboard**.

**wizard**   A specialized template that asks you questions about what type of document you want to create, and then generates the document for you based on your answers.

**zoom**   To change the magnification of a document onscreen. You can zoom in to enlarge a document or zoom out to shrink it.

# A

# B

**commands**

# D

**data sources (mail merge)**
creating, 190-191
adding, 192-193
editing, 192
**Date and Time command
(Insert menu), 148**
**Date/Time Properties dialog
box, 149**
**dates**
documents, adding, 148-149
fields, 148-149
footers, inserting, 132
headers, inserting, 132
wrong, 149
**deactivating automatic
grammar checker, 141**
**decimal tabs, setting, 110-111**
**default margins, 122-123**
**default tabs, restoring, 112**
**Delete command (Table
menu), 161**
**Delete key, 50**
**deleting**
columns in tables, 165-166
custom tabs, 112-113
multiple items (Clipboard), 59
rows in tables, 165-166

shortcuts to Favorites
folder, 71
tables, 161
text, 50
accidental, 33
**dialog boxes**
Borders and Shading, 115
Create AutoText, 153
Create Labels, 201
Date/Time Properties, 149
Edit Hyperlink, 204
Envelopes and Labels, 88
Find, 78
Format Picture, 179
function of, 14
Insert ClipArt, 175
Insert Hyperlink, 205
Label Options, 201
Labels Options, 90
New, 72
Office Assistant, 25
Page Setup, 126
Paragraph, 102
Print, 14-15, 86
Spelling and Grammar, 142
Symbol, 146
Zoom, 8
**displaying**
context menus, 12
hidden symbols in docu-
ments, 61

Office Clipboard, 59
Picture toolbar, 179
**docking floating toolbars,
20-22**
**documents**
click and type feature, 36
closing, 66-67
columns
formatting, 158-159
inserting, 156-157
length of, 159
number of, 156
text hyphenation, 159
width of, 158
converting from Web pages,
208-209
creating, 72-73
dates, adding, 148-149
Favorites folder, accessing,
70-71
footers
adding, 130-131
date insertion, 132
page number insertion, 132
graphics
adding, 174-175
cropping, 178-179
moving, 176-177
sizing, 176-177
text-wrapping options, 176,
180-181

**documents**

# E

portrait orientation (documents), 123

previewing Web pages in browsers, 207

**Print button (Standard toolbar), 86**

**Print command (File menu), 15, 86**

**Print dialog box, 14-16, 86**

**Print Layout command (View menu), 36, 82**

**Print Layout view versus Normal view, 82**

**Print Preview**
  closing, 85
  multiple page view, 84
  page breaks, 124
  page up/down buttons, 84
  paper waste, 84
  Shrink to Fit button, 84

**printer fonts, 97**

**printers**
  documents, printing, 86-87
  pages per sheet setting, 87
  Print Preview feature, 84

**printing**
  documents, 86-87
    multiple copies, 87
    pages per sheet, 87
  envelopes, 88-89
    mail merge, 198-199

help topics, 27

labels, 90
  mail merge, 200-201
  page ranges in documents, 87

**producing form letters (mail merge), 196-197**

**Programs command (Start menu), 4**

**pull-down menus**
  command functionality, 8-10
  versus toolbars, 8, 16

# R

**records (data sources)**
  adding (mail merge), 192-193
  editing (mail merge), 192

**red wavy lines, automatic spell checking, 140**

**Redo button (Standard toolbar), 53**

**removing**
  borders
    from graphics, 179
    from paragraphs, 115
  color from text, 99
  highlighted text, 99
  hyperlinks, 204
  tabs in documents, 60
  toolbar buttons, 19

**Replace command (Edit menu), 138**

**replacing**
  text in documents, 42, 138-139
  words, synonym options (Thesaurus), 144-145

**resizing**
  columns in tables, 165
  fonts, 97
  graphics, 176-177
  rows in tables, 165
  tables, 167
  windows, 6

**restoring default tabs, 112**

**right tabs, setting, 108-109**

**rows (tables)**
  adding, 164
  deleting, 165-166
  resizing, 165

**Ruler command (View menu), 10, 14**

**rulers, hiding, 13**

# S

**Save As Web Page command (File menu), 206**

**Save button (Standard toolbar), 64**